PEOPLE'S GOVERNOR

My Internship Experience with
Lt.Governor Dr. Kiran Bedi

Foreword by
Hon'ble Justice P.S Dinesh Kumar

KRITHIK KAILASH

CONTENTS

Dr. Kiran Bedi
Lieutenant Governor

Raj Nivas
Puducherry

No.6/LGS/HH/2019   *20th November 2019*

C E R T I F I C A T E

This is to certify that

Krithik Kailash

Student, BA LLB, I year, Christ University, Bengaluru

has interned at the Raj Nivas, Puducherry from 20.10.2019 to 20.11.2019 as part of the Youth Engagement Programme.

During this period, Krithik Kailash worked on following modules.

- *Jal Shakti Abhiyan –*
  Mission Water Rich Puducherry | Mission Green Puducherry
- *Outreach Programmes – Rural Education | Field Visits*
- *Research and Data Analysis*
- *Assistance to the Video Team*
- *Office Management Systems*

Mr. Krithik Kailash is an excellent team player with an eye for detail.

With Best Wishes,

Dr. Kiran Bedi

Dr. Kiran Bedi
Lieutenant Governor

Raj Nivas
Puducherry 605 001
Phone : *0413 2334050*
Fax : *0413 2334025*
E-mail : *lg.pon@nic.in*

No. 6/LGS/HH/2021   February 16, 2021

CERTIFICATE
****

This is to place on record appreciation for the work done by **Krithik Kailash,** Student, BA LLB 1 year, Christ University, Bengaluru during his Internship Programme with this office from 03rd February 2021 to 16th February 2021.

During this period, he handled the following work profiles:

1. A Compilation and Research on The Revitalization of Kanagan Lake - towards the collaborative research work taken up with the University of Southampton as part of Mission Water Rich.

2. Compilation of news clippings on Water Rich Puducherry and Weekend Rounds 2016 to 2020.

3. Intern Lecture Series.

4. On the Field Visits: Auroville | Velrampet Lake.

5. Outreach Program – Rural Education.

Mr. Krithik Kailash is a conscientious team member.

With best wishes,

Dr. Kiran Bedi

Justice P.S Dinesh Kumar
Judge,
High Court of Karnataka

12 July, 2023

FOREWORD

This humble yet striking book is about a young, energetic and smart budding lawyer's experience of his training under the mentorship of the illustrious Dr. Kiran Bedi. At a young age, Mr. Krithik Kailash has added an important feather to his cap of authoring such a credible book. The experiences he has gathered as a mentee is not limited as it gives the reader a chance to understand this young mind's perseverance to learn and excel with such honesty.

This book speaks about Dr. Kiran Bedi's life from a tender age when the Indian Police Service made a distinct and positive mark on her mind which led her to become the first woman IPS officer rising to the rank of Director General. Her notable service continued even at the United Nations as an advisor of Police. The author rightly calls her a 'Global Cop' in this book. This promising officer has not proved her mettle in the Police department as merely a Police officer but also has displayed a humane side by reforming and rehabilitating prisoners at Tihar jail which rendered her the prestigious Ramon Magsasay award.

The author has been fortunate to be guided under the Raj Nivas Youth Engagement Program launched in 2017, an uplifting program for the young minds of the nation. He has keenly spoken about all his learnings under Dr. Kiran Bedi as the Lieutenant Governor of Puducherry highlighting two important aspects. Firstly that 'Raj Nivas'; residence of the Governor, during the tenure of Dr. Kiran Bedi was open to every citizen without any discrimination and secondly that her tenure witnessed a transformation pillared by a mission of accessibility, transparency, and collaboration. This program has empowered the author in different ways by giving an opportunity to gain theoretical and practical experience by travelling extensively for visioned projects with Dr. Bedi and team such as Mission Green Puducherry, Water Rich Puducherry, Namme Neer Karaikal, Sitheri Channel Walk and several other outreach programmes. These projects are for the good of the land, nature and humanity at large which are necessary for a sustainable evolution of this world. Conservation of resources, protection of the land, improving the existing eco-system and saving it from contamination in order to pass it on for the future has been strongly taught to these young minds in these programs. This has become excessively important after the onslaught of a virus called Covid. The timeline now is divided as pre and post Covid era. The author has also brought to the readers as to how Dr. Bedi relentlessly worked during such testing times and offered her services to help the country in this fight against Covid.

This program has also opened the doors for the young and brilliant minds to gather significant memories from working for such dedicated causes as well as meeting coveted people of the country which is highly important to broaden one's horizon and to understand life at a deeper level.

The author had a goal-oriented vision that he would reach the gates of Raj Nivas so definitively and he ultimately manifested the same for himself with his hard work and talent. But more importantly, Mr. Krithik Kailash has earned the blessings of Bhagawan Shri Perumal and HanumanJi who have undoubtedly blessed this capable, bright, destined young man to achieve greater success ahead for himself. I also take this opportunity to congratulate the young, bright Mr. Krithik Kailash and pray Bhagawan Shri Krishna to bless him immensely in all his endeavours in life and convey my greetings on authoring his maiden book.

(P.S Dinesh Kumar)

Justice P.S Dinesh Kumar
Judge, High Court of Karnataka

ACKNOWLEDGEMENT

Acknowledgment ensures the presence of personalities who made this book a reality for the scholarly world. I deem it a privilege and great fortune to have received the blessings of His Lordship Hon'ble Justice P.S Dinesh Kumar in the form of a foreword.

I express my gratitude to Lt. Governor Dr. Kiran Bedi for imparting essential leadership lessons for life. Every day of observation provided me with insights into the unstoppable governance administered by the Lt. Governor.

I am deeply indebted to Puducherry's renowned Comptroller Mrs. Asha Gupta, for enabling me to craft each page of the book with divine guidance.

In the first week of March 2017, my parents, Dr. Kathirvel and Mrs. Arthy Lakshmi, took me to Puducherry as part of Visitor's Hour to meet the Lt. Governor. This visit sparked the idea of interning at Raj Nivas. The sacrifice and determination of my parents to provide quality education to their children have pillared our progress for over two decades on Planet Earth.

I'm thankful to my teachers and friends for being a constant source of strength and support throughout the process of completing this book.

Lastly, I'd like to express my appreciation to Notion Press for their creative ideas in publishing this book.

Krithik Kailash

ABOUT THE AUTHOR

Outreach with children

Krithik Kailash, an undergraduate law student at Christ University, received the 'Best Orator of the Year' award during his schooling at Sarala Birla Academy. In September 2019, he felt a strong desire for mentorship, leading him to intern at the office of Puducherry's Lieutenant Governor Dr. Kiran Bedi. He worked extensively on initiatives such as Jal Shakti Abhiyan, Mission Water Rich Puducherry, Mission Green Puducherry, Outreach Programs – Rural education, and field visits.

Kailash's reading habits are extensive, with the Bhagavad Gita deeply influencing his perspective on leading a purposeful life. He attributes his strong values of spirituality and inner strength to his parents, for which he is grateful. Additionally, Kailash is enthusiastic about playing both tennis and football.

Dr. Kiran Bedi, the Lieutenant Governor, described Kailash as a 'young man of character and strong value systems' in a tweet shared across various social media platforms. Currently, Kailash is interning at the Chambers of Hon'ble Justice P.S Dinesh Kumar at the Karnataka High Court. In the foreword of this book 'People's Governor,' Justice P.S Dinesh Kumar describes him as a 'young, energetic, and smart budding lawyer.'

At the age of twenty-one, Kailash is about to publish his first book, which documents his lifetime experiences as an intern at the office of Lieutenant Governor Dr. Kiran Bedi.

NOTE ON INTERNSHIP

"A position does not define a person, but a person defines the position. Dr. Kiran Bedi defined the position of the Lt. Governor of Puducherry"

– By Krithik Kailash

My internship confirmation from the Lieutenant Governor's office led me to the gates of Raj Nivas on October 20th, 2019. The woman guard at the entrance of Raj Nivas mentioned that I could take a picture with Lieutenant Governor Dr. Kiran Bedi, along with an autograph. Content with the guard's words, I expected a brief meeting with the Lt. Governor.

My work at the office of the Lt. Governor is now part of the pages of history books.

I experienced the eternal presence of Maharishi Aurobindo Ghosh and Divine Mother Mirra Alfassa. The functioning of the Aurobindo Integral Education and Auroville Society provided me with insights into the inner world of Puducherry. French Architecture has a unique place in India's historical past. I connected with Mother nature's beauty bestowed upon the land of Puducherry through extensive fieldwork undertaken to fulfill the mission of 'Prosperous Puducherry.' A stroll along the picturesque beaches is a must for citizens travelling to the Union Territory. The chants of Brahmananda Swaroopa by Sadhguru echoed through the residence of the Lt. Governor. I worked in a spiritually charged atmosphere merged with infinite time.

Connecting with citizens and students broadened my understanding of societal transformation. Collaborating with Government departments and meeting the Collector of Karaikal gave me an eagle's eye into the multifaceted aspects of administrative governance. I worked beyond the regular office hours in the room assigned to interns. Some days, work extended until 11.30 PM, and if it ended by 6 PM, I volunteered to stay longer to enjoy the precious moments within the Governor's Palace.

I have endeavored to present my work as an intern at Raj Nivas in a simple and forthright manner for the benefit of readers. I aim to impact the student community by awakening their inner potential for dedicating themselves to 'work' from a young age, continually learning to enhance their individual talent. This book aims to inspire young minds to channel their energy for the welfare of our motherland. Documenting my experiences and learnings in the upcoming chapters extensively covers personal writings and prepared reports during the internship.

Lt. Governor Dr. Kiran Bedi is renowned as a fearless police officer. I witnessed the motherly side of Lt. Governor in ensuring the academic progress of interns at Raj Nivas. I sincerely hope that each of you enjoy reading the book as you travel through my time as an intern at the Office of Lt. Governor.

18th July 2023   **Krithik Kailash**

Tamil Nadu

Chapter 1

JOURNEY TO SUCCESS

Picture of Dr. Kiran Bedi

The life of Dr. Kiran Bedi has inspired people in India and across the world. From being a tennis champion to becoming India's first woman to join the Indian Police Service, the life of the 24th Lt. Governor of Puducherry is a journey through challenges. A symbol of hope and courage for countless Indians. My research into Dr. Kiran Bedi's life provided astounding details for a comprehensive study of the turning points which laid the foundations for a successful career in the Indian Police Service. Below, I have attached the elaborate report prepared during my internship at the office of the Lt. Governor to benefit the readers.

TURNING POINT – 1:

At the age of 8, a significant turning point came in the life of Dr. Kiran Bedi. A woman ran to their house and asked for help from Dr. Kiran Bedi's father, saying, "Babuji, I want your help. Please help me." The woman's husband had been arrested, and she believed he was innocent. Dr. Kiran Bedi's father was convinced that the woman needed help, as she had been a neighbor for many years. This was the first introduction to a profession called the Police. Dr. Kiran Bedi's father called up the Senior Superintendent of Police and requested him to listen to the woman's plight, saying, "If she is right, then please ensure that no injustice is done to her." Importantly, Dr. Kiran Bedi's father didn't demand the man's release; instead, he connected the woman with the person who had the capacity to address the injustice. This incident continued to impact Dr. Kiran Bedi and highlighted two important messages:

a)   The Police department can undo injustice

b)   The importance of being in a position to help people.

This realization had a positive effect on Dr. Kiran Bedi who realized the influence and power of the police in rendering justice.

Kiran saw our father make a phone call to the area officer for fair intervention.
Officer, if this man is innocent, please ensure no injustice is done to him
And it worked!! By evening, the lady's husband was back home!

God, please help me be in a position of influence to help people in need!

TURNING POINT – 2:

The second turning point in the life of Dr. Kiran Bedi was a result of her parents' emphasis on sports and education. In those days, dowry was not considered an offence; the Dowry Act was introduced much later after Independence in the year 1961. The more elaborate the display of dowry, the wealthier the parents were perceived to be, and grander the wedding feast. Dr. Kiran Bedi's parents often took her to such weddings, where clothes, sarees, and valuable items were showcased. However, it was never expressly mentioned that these items were demanded. Dr. Kiran Bedi took a stand against this practice and expressed rejection to her father by saying, "This will never happen in my life. I won't let you go through this, and you won't have to give me away with dowry." This moment marked a significant shift in her personal beliefs as a woman, as she evolved and gained a deeper understanding of the meaning of marriage, parenting, and work leading to the second turning point in the life of Dr. Kiran Bedi.

TURNING POINT - 3:

Dr. Kiran Bedi became the National Junior Tennis champion at the age of 16 when a girl from Amritsar defeated India's number 1 player. At that time, Wimbledon's rule stated that the National Junior Tennis Champion earned a seat in Wimbledon. However, vested interests in the Tennis Association denied her this well-deserved opportunity, even though she had earned it through merit. This incident made Dr. Kiran Bedi realize that sports could not be the career path. Instead, she decided to focus on academics, as it would allow her to be independent in choosing a future based on her interests and passions.

This was also the time where public administration and joining the Government became a goal in Dr. Kiran Bedi's life. The firm belief that dedicated focus and energy into academics will take her to the Union Public Service Commission indeed materialized in the later years. Mother India saw its daughter becoming the first woman to join the Indian Police Service.

TURNING POINT – 4:

Dr. Kiran Bedi has always been a firm believer in reformation, preparation, and prevention. Every time while arresting a person as a police officer. Dr. Kiran Bedi would find out - why did he commit the crime? How could I help him so that he doesn't repeat the crime? As a young police officer, Dr. Kiran Bedi was keen on correcting and reforming individuals over time, so they wouldn't resort to crime again. The reformation of the individual by working with his family and children showed the importance of Socio - Justice Criminal System of reform and rehabilitation. It was during her posting as Inspector General of Prisons that her career took a significant turn. Dr. Kiran Bedi, being a reformer, preventer, and a sociologist at heart, knew she was heading to the right place where she could make a real difference.

TURNING POINT - 5:

As the IG of Tihar Prisons, Dr. Kiran Bedi reformed thousands of prisoners, including those she had previously sent to jail during her tenure as DCP - West and Deputy Commissioner of Police - North. The strong belief in prevention and rehabilitation led to the introduction of educational reforms and meditation programs within the prison. Tihar Prison was administered to meet the needs of its 10,000 residents, mirroring a well-functioning township. The implementation of spiritual programs, medical care, and collaboration with Indira Gandhi Open University for educational reforms were all pivotal moments. These efforts emphasized the importance of rewarding prevention and cemented the notion that Prevention is as crucial as Detection in policing.

Dr. Kiran Bedi's approach humanized policing, evident by her being the first police officer worldwide to receive the esteemed Ramon Magsaysay Award. The award recognized a new model of collaborative approach and dedication in working with the community for the betterment of society. It showcased the significance of humane, rehabilitative, and corrective policing. The Ramon Magsaysay Award proved to be a significant turning point, providing visibility and acclaim for reformative policing. Following this honour, Dr. Kiran Bedi was invited to have breakfast with President Clinton at the White House, further acknowledging her exceptional contributions.

Receiving the Ramon Magsaysay Award, equivalent to the Asian Nobel Prize in Manila in 1994

TURNING POINT – 6:

The next significant turning point in Dr. Kiran Bedi's career was her appointment as the Police Advisor at the United Nations in 2003. This prestigious international selection was a testament to the collaborative policing approach, which encompassed prevention, correction, rehabilitation, and restoration – in line with the UN's policies on Criminal Justice. As the first woman in the world to hold the position of Police Advisor at the UN, Dr. Kiran Bedi took charge of overseeing 30 Peace Keeping Missions in countries like Sudan, Liberia, Congo, Somalia, Cyprus, and Kosovo – nations that are gradually finding stability today. The invaluable lessons from successful policing systems in these regions were brought back by Dr. Kiran Bedi, earning her the title of a "Global Cop". Despite having the opportunity to continue her service at the UN, Dr. Kiran Bedi made the heartfelt decision to return back to Mother India. Cherishing every moment of the 'Indianship' - The kind of freedom, democracy and opportunities in Dr. Kiran Bedi's words are 'unparalleled' in our country.

As the Police Advisor to Secretary-General, United Nations (New York) on Peace Keeping Operations, 2003-2005

TURNING POINT - 7:

The position of Lieutenant Governor of Puducherry marked the next distinguished step in Dr. Kiran Bedi's life, bringing all her administrative experience to benefit the region. As the First Citizen of Puducherry, overseeing the entire territory became a turning point for her. Dr. Kiran Bedi opened up Raj Nivas to everyone, making it accessible to people from all walks of life – be it a child, a rich person, an elderly individual, or anyone else. This approach to governance set a model for the entire country, demonstrating that high office and position are meant to connect with the common person and bridge the gap with the highest office in the territory.

The management of the Covid pandemic and Cyclone showcased the importance of collaborative work, with all agencies and departments working together seamlessly. Dr. Kiran Bedi's ability to network with people every day through multimedia and technology played a crucial role in connecting with the last person and addressing their concerns. Fondly known as the People's Governor by the citizens, her tenure transformed Raj Nivas and the administration, characterized by accessibility, transparency, and collaboration.

Chapter 2

INNER CALLING

Picture from the Official Website of Lt. Governor

In 2019, as my first internship period approached, I listened to my classmates discuss their plans while I was still uncertain about the nature of my training. I began to recognize the presence of clues and patterns in students' lives that guide us to climb each step with confidence and conviction. Dr. APJ Abdul Kalam's extensive mention of the experiences gained from influential figures like Dr. Vikram Sarabhai and Professor Satish Dhawan in the field of space science inspired me. I firmly believed that my internship should be under the mentorship of a great personality.

During my search for a book to read in the Autobiography/Biography section of our school's library in 2014, I came across a particular book that caught my attention. The cover featured a police officer with a determined look, and in bold letters, it read 'I DARE.' It resonated with me, and my inner voice urged me to travel to Puducherry and meet Dr. Kiran Bedi. This curiosity led me to explore the possibility of interning at Raj Nivas, Puducherry.

Upon confirmation from Mrs. Asha Gupta, the Comptroller of Raj Nivas, I was thrilled to begin my internship from 20th October 2019 to 21st November 2019. The official website of Raj Nivas, Puducherry, provided the following details about the internship:

"The Raj Nivas which is now the official office and residence of Lt. Governor has been standing tall, with its impressive French Architecture, since 1766. Under the visionary leadership of Her Excellency, the Lt. Governor of Puducherry, Dr. Kiran Bedi, the Raj Nivas opened its doors to young millennials for the first time in its illustrious history. The Raj Nivas Youth Engagement program was launched in 2017 with the aim of nurturing and building leaders for the nation."

YOUTH ENGAGEMENT PROGRAM:

The Youth Engagement Program aims to foster public service and leadership skills while providing a unique opportunity to equip students with valuable professional experience in nation-building - New India. The interns receive hands-on mentoring to strengthen their understanding of the Executive role of Raj Nivas and its mission to serve the people of Puducherry and the Nation.

As an intern, the assignments on any given day could include conducting research, creating analytical reports, documentation, understanding dynamics, attending meetings & briefings, creating & updating presentations and fact sheets, managing social media communication, participating in open house events, engaging in public relations, interacting with visitors, contributing to social outreach programs, working on service & eco-oriented projects, liaising with schools, colleges, NGOs, and even conceptualizing to manage events. The program provides a diverse range of experiences, allowing interns to make meaningful contributions to the community and develop a spirit of service and leadership.

WAY FORWARD:

The next step is to take the Youth Engagement Program to college campuses nationwide. This will enable us to tap into the potential of the best Civil services aspirants, students of Political Science, Sociology, Law, and active youth leaders. The idea is to "Catch them young" and introduce 'Short Volunteer Programs' for students between 14-17 years, acquainting them with conscious and purposeful governance.

My decision to intern at Raj Nivas, Puducherry, proved to be a transformative moment in my life. It provided me with the best learning experience, and each opportunity as an intern at Raj Nivas was a valuable learning curve. Every interaction with Dr. Kiran Bedi remains vivid in my mind.

During the internship, good values and moral education played a fundamental role, shaping our outlook with curiosity and a desire for constant learning. The internship training focused on constructive, experiential, cooperative, and collaborative learning, carefully crafted by Team Raj Nivas to foster holistic development among interns. We learned that education becomes complete when a person truly understands oneself and connects with the world. As Maharishi Aurobindo eloquently notes, the chief aim of education should be to help the growing soul draw out its best qualities and make them perfect for noble use. This philosophy guided our internship training, promoting personal growth and a sense of purpose in contributing to society.

Chapter 3

WORK ON DAY ONE

Left to Right: Grandfather Sivam, Grandmother Shakuntala Sivam, Mother Mrs. Arthy Lakshmi, Lt. Governor Dr. Kiran Bedi, Myself, Comptroller of Raj Nivas Mrs. Asha Gupta and Chief Grievance Officer Dr. Bascarane.

On Monday afternoon, 21st October 2019, I entered the majestic office of the Lieutenant Governor of Puducherry. Dr. Kiran Bedi warmly greeted my family members and me as I walked in. After lunch, the first half of work involved documenting news clippings, followed by the delightful task of organizing the personal library of the Lieutenant Governor in a systematic manner. While categorizing and rearranging the books, to my amazement, Dr. Kiran Bedi entered the room.

I was astonished for two reasons:

a. I had the privilege of accessing the residence of the Lieutenant Governor.

b. Dr. Kiran Bedi acknowledged me with a smile and instructed her personal staff to ensure my comfort while working.

It felt like a divine blessing to begin my first day of work by dutifully arranging the extensive collection of books in the personal library of Lieutenant Governor. In the following days, I learned that accessibility to Raj Nivas by the common man was a fundamental principle of governance for Dr. Kiran Bedi.

GOVERNOR'S PALACE BECAME A PEOPLE'S PALACE.

Picture of Namakkal' s Lord Anjaneya to Lt. Governor Dr. Kiran Bedi

Father – Dr. Kathirvel with Lt. Governor Dr. Kiran Bedi [2017]

Chapter 4

PREPARE TO PERFORM

Lt. Governor Dr. Kiran Bedi interacts with Interns on Good Governance

My detailed study on Trust, Empowerment, and Accountability (TEA) provided valuable insights into the governance mantra delivered by the Lieutenant Governor on 29th May 2016 as part of the inaugural address to the people of Puducherry. This mantra laid the foundation for a vision towards a "Prosperous Puducherry." Dr. Kiran Bedi and Team Raj Nivas meticulously planned to make the Union Territory of Puducherry prosperous. During my internship, I learned that the first day of meetings with government officials involved conducting a Strength, Weakness, Opportunity, and Threat (SWOT) analysis for Puducherry. This analysis identified the strengths, weaknesses, and opportunities, leading to the formulation of the five pillars of true governance. The Lieutenant Governor established the five pillars of the True Governance Model - Invite, Involve, Resolve, Solve, and Evolve. This model, propounded by Dr. Kiran Bedi, became the guiding light in transforming 'Raj Nivas' into 'People's Nivas.' I gave an elaborate presentation after conducting detailed research on each of the five pillars, which I will now elaborate below:

- **The first pillar - 'Invite'** – began by opening the doors of Raj Nivas to all sections of society. The lawns of Raj Nivas became venues for open-air theaters and cinema, where people from different walks of life came together to celebrate various festivals and participate in events, transforming Raj Nivas into 'Seva Nivas | People Nivas.' Notable visitors included the President of India and other eminent dignitaries.

- **The second pillar of True Governance is 'Involve'** – Involvement of the Lieutenant Governor, the Secretariat, and private participation led to initiatives such as beach cleaning, prison reforms and dengue prevention. The involvement of the people led a People's Movement in Puducherry, aiming to make the region water-rich, green, and clean, ensuring a quality life for its residents. The combined efforts of the People, Corporates, and NGOs resulted in Mission Green Puducherry, Water Rich Puducherry, and Swachh Puducherry to sustain our ecosystem.

- **The third pillar of True Governance is 'Resolve'** – The Open House system effectively addresses people's grievances, allowing individuals to submit petitions to the Lt. Governor. Every petition is documented, analyzed, and attended to make governance accessible and responsive. Weekend morning rounds saw the Lt. Governor and Team Raj Nivas collaborating with the public to clean lakes and ponds. Surprise inspections of police stations, healthcare centers, and children's homes form another aspect of the third pillar, focusing on resolving issues effectively.

- **The fourth pillar of True Governance is 'Solve'** – The Mission Water Rich Puducherry aimed to address the water crisis in the region. The Lieutenant Governor and Team Raj Nivas, with the support of Corporates as part of their social responsibility, worked tirelessly to desilt canals and ensure the free flow of water. This mission significantly increased the water table in Puducherry with the Lieutenant Governor duly recognizing the efforts of donors for their noble contribution in making water accessible to all. In the Medical Seats issue, the Lieutenant Governor Dr. Kiran Bedi, intervened to protect the students' interests. The CBI investigation recommended by the Lieutenant Governor and the judgements by judiciary brought an end to this issue. The Lieutenant Governor ensured a shift from distributing free rice to Direct Bank Transfers of money to beneficiaries underscores the importance of the fourth pillar in True Governance - 'Solve', finding solutions to challenges even in the face of adversity.

- **The fifth pillar of True Governance is 'Evolve'** – The list of file dispositions was made public using various communication methods, ensuring transparency, and keeping everyone informed about the status of files. Weekly messages and documented publications contributed to institutional memory and evolved as hallmarks of transparent administration. Dr. Kiran Bedi introduced the acronym IIRSE (Invite | Involve | Resolve | Solve | Evolve) to the citizens of Puducherry, encouraging them to 'I RISE'. This emphasizes the significance of developing Emotional Quotient (EQ) and Spiritual Quotient (SQ) alongside Intelligence Quotient (IQ) for wholesome individual leadership.

Field Work as part of Mission Green Puducherry

'Involve' – A Pillar of True Governance

MISSION WATER-RICH PUDUCHERRY

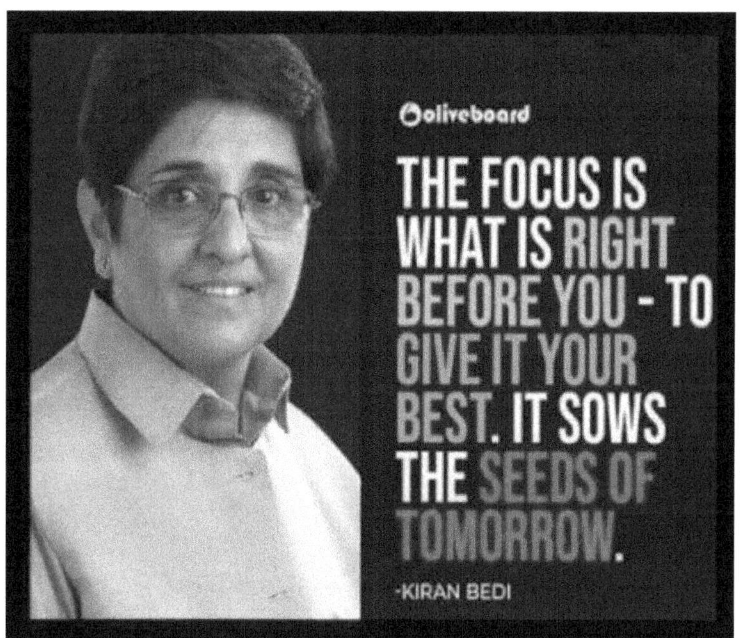

Quote of Dr. Kiran Bedi

I worked extensively on the Water Rich model which led to the rejuvenation of water bodies in Puducherry. There was a strong coordination amongst all agencies. It was a collaborative effort between the Public Works Department, Department of Industries, Agriculture Department, and Municipality with the support of the people, leading to the evolution of a community-driven effort led by the Lieutenant Governor. I was tasked to document the desilted sites across the region of Puducherry.

I began the work to document a short film on the extraordinary collaborative work between the Lt. Governor and the people of Puducherry. The work started at 6.30 AM along with the presence of the concerned CSR donors at the site of work.

The field visits provided me with important lessons such as;

PLANNING IS THE KEY TO SUCCESS:

The plan for Mission Water Rich Puducherry began with the objective of rejuvenating all water bodies, including water tanks, lakes, ponds, and canals. The ultimate goal was to ensure a surplus of drinking water for the residents of Puducherry thereby enhancing their quality of life. The mission aimed to rejuvenate 23 water channels along with more than 600 lakes and ponds. The desilting of the first canal commenced on 29th September 2018 and since then, the work had been in full swing with the vision of making Puducherry water-rich for many years to come.

TACKLING THE CHALLENGES:

At one point, the Public Works Department (PWD) acknowledged that they lacked the necessary funds to cover the cost of desilting 86 kilometers of 23 feeder channels, as well as desilting and maintaining 84 tanks and 609 ponds. Recognizing the urgency of the situation, the Lt. Governor appealed to the community at large, making the first such appeal through Twitter, which received an instant response. Corporate support started flowing in response to appeals for desilting water canals and tanks. Team Raj Nivas along with other officials, dedicated several weekends to morning rounds to continually inspect the progress of the mission. This persistent effort proved crucial in overcoming potential obstacles and ensuring the success of mission water rich.

DESILTING OF:

Rural Water Bodies   *Drains across the city*   *Weekend visits to Ponds*

WATER - THE SOURCE OF ALL LIFE:

Throughout history, water has played a crucial role in the emergence of civilizations. However, according to UN statistics, approximately 2.5 billion people lack access to safe drinking water and around one billion people do not have access to a reliable water source. The Mission Water Rich Puducherry successfully addressed this issue by desilting 86 kilometers of water channels and rejuvenating over 600 lakes and ponds that were previously drying up. There had been an increase in the ground water level which were previously low due to the blockade of water.

A field study was conducted by a Raj Nivas Intern studying in the Harvard University. In this field study it was analyzed that all the farmers who were interviewed had positively responded to Mission Water Rich Puducherry. They specifically mentioned that there has been a steady rise in their income as there is more availability of the water due to the desilting of channels. The farmers also acknowledged that the desilting of the channels had led to the prevention of flooding in their fields due to heavy rainfall that used to destroy their crops. A resident of Villianur, enthusiastically mentioned to us that the desilting has immensely benefitted them as it had ensured that there is adequate water supply to the people. The Mission Water Rich Puducherry helped in improving the agricultural productivity in the region and extended its reach to urban and semi – urban drains besides water – ways.

SUSTAINABLE DEVELOPMENT:

The Mission Water Rich Puducherry also facilitated compliance with rainwater harvesting rules for local industries, resulting in significant water conservation. Companies began setting up and updating rainwater harvesting structures periodically under the guidance of the concerned authority. The enthusiastic support and involvement of Resident Welfare Associations, NGOs, schools, and local workers demonstrated that a community-driven effort is essential for a sustainable and liveable planet. The unique initiative of Public-Private participation showcased successful collaboration across platforms.

WATER-RICH PUDUCHERRY IN TIMES OF EXTREME SCARCITY:

The Jal Shakti Abhiyan was launched by the Ministry of Jal Shakti in 2019. A campaign for water conservation and water security in the country through a collaborative effort of various ministries of the Government of India and State Governments. The Mission Water Rich Puducherry resulted in achieving the goals envisioned by the Government of India to ensure that there is sufficient water for the people of Puducherry. The initiative implemented by Dr. Kiran Bedi is a unique model that can make our entire country water rich for the coming generations. Water Rich Puducherry is a success story of Government of India's Jal Shakti Abhiyan initiative.

The Mission Water Rich Puducherry remains to be the largest water movement in the history of Puducherry. We documented the work by visiting a number of desilted channels apart from lakes and ponds as part of the documentation for Swachhata Hi Seva award ceremony. I firmly believed that Mission Water Rich should continue as a people's movement which will eventually lead to the rejuvenation of several other water bodies in the region. It is important to create awareness by conducting channel walks for understanding the simple means through which we can conserve water. As an Intern at Raj Nivas, I was able to realize the impact which the channel walks have had on the minds of children as it gave them the best learning experience possible for a student. Mission Water Rich Puducherry succeeded despite several challenges and obstacles with the objective to have abundant water for its people, ushering prosperity and happiness to the residents.

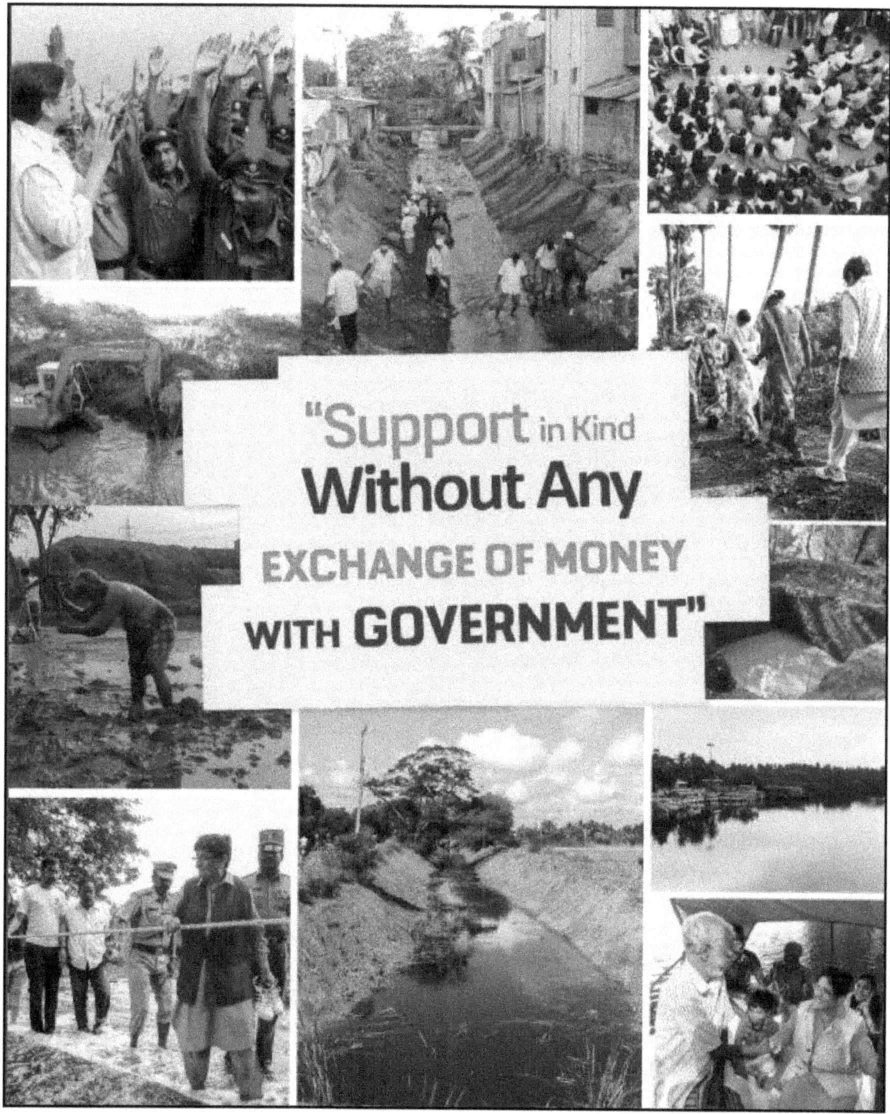

Desilted Pandhasozhanallur Tank Feeding Channel at Nettapakkam village

Lake cleaned as part of Lt. Governor' s Mission Water Rich

RURAL CHANNELS 2019 — DONOR GALLERY

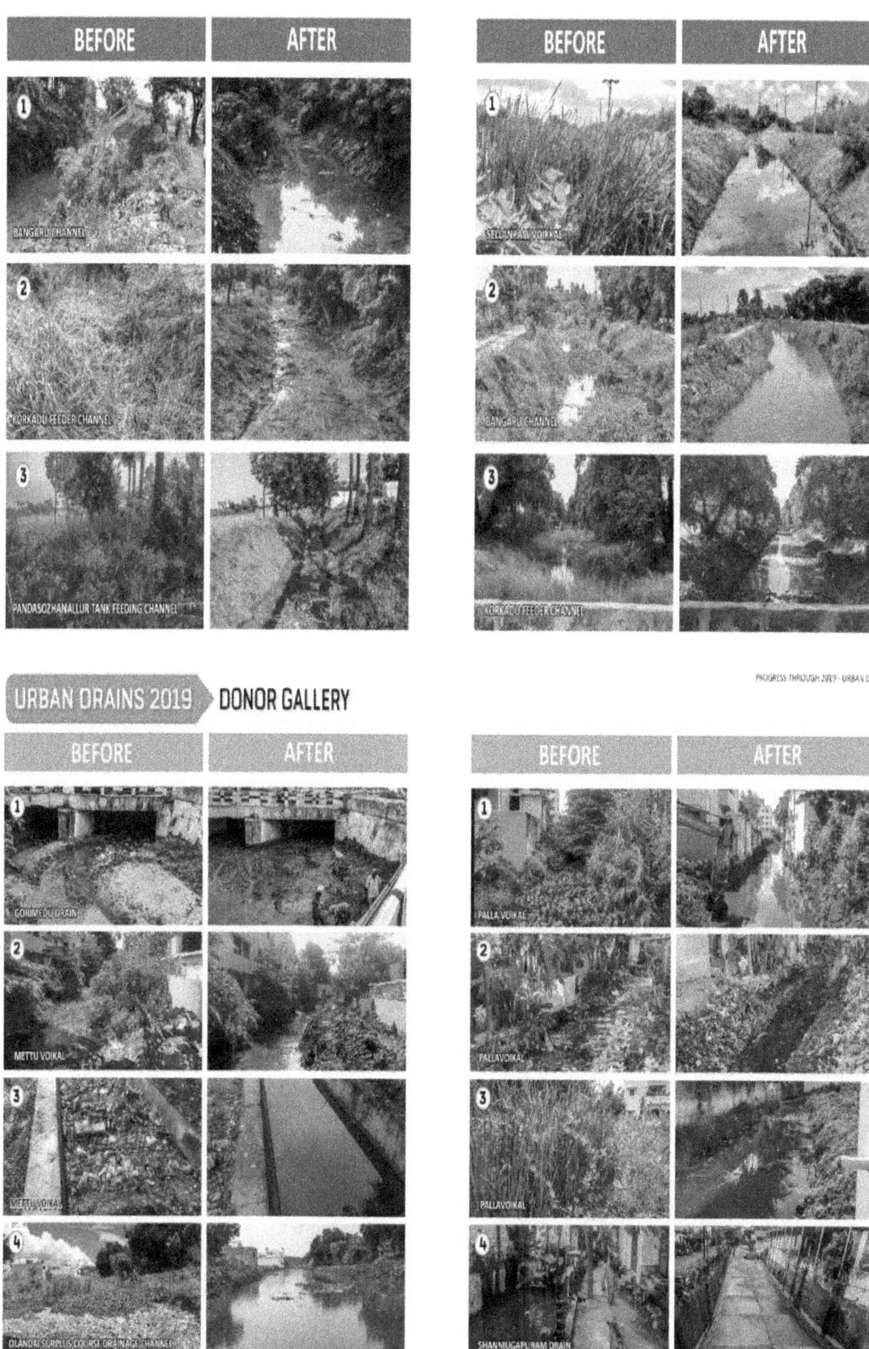

URBAN DRAINS 2019 — DONOR GALLERY

THE RESOLVE

Kiran Bedi @thekiranbedi

Coming together to make Puducherry 'Rich In Water'... Together we identified possible impediments and resolved to work together. In the pic are the Honorable Ministers, senior public officials and activists from NGOs, Academia, and concerned citizens. @AshwaniKumar_92

23 Mar 2018

THE FIRST VISIT

SENSITISING THE COMMUNITY

Kiran Bedi @thekiranbedi

Weekend morning round 147 Visit to Manalipet village Sankarabarani river bed. All together, Public officials' with *@ishafoundation* and *@AOLSwamiji* organisation volunteers to work at Micro & Macro level to make Puducherry Rich in Water. @PMOIndia @drharshvardhan @AshwaniKumar_92

The team also inspected factories & universities located in the areas with alarmingly low ground water levels. The identified water guzzling industries and institutions were asked to replenish their reserve within campuses or adopt a near-by village pond.

Kiran Bedi @thekiranbedi

08 JUL 2018

Team #WaterRich Puducherry on its way to inspect water recharrge systems. All together in a bus. Chief Engineer, Hydrologist, Science and technology Commune Commisioner, Chief Town Planner and the planning authority. Coming together converts individuals into empowered team .

Chapter 6

TRAVEL TO KARAIKAL

In Collaboration with the Community

The 236th Morning Round was scheduled for Karaikal, a region of Puducherry, as part of the Mission Water Rich and Green Puducherry. Lieutenant Governor Dr. Kiran Bedi reviewed the work done by the Karaikal Collectorate and expressed gratitude to the people of Karaikal by planting more trees. During my visit, I observed the desilting of ponds around Karaikal including the review of the Aayikulam Pond and the desilting works undertaken by educational institutions. I intend to share the historical significance of the Aayikulam pond, which holds a special place in Puducherry's history. Situated at Muthirapalayam, Oulgaret Municipality, Puducherry, the Aayikulam pond was built by a Devadasi named Aayi, who was an influential philanthropist of her times. According to legends, Krishna Devaraya, the King of Vijayanagara, was passing through Ozhukarai (Oulgaret) and mistook Aayi's well-lit house for a temple. He offered prayers there but later realized it was the residence of Aayi, a Devadasi. In response to this revelation, Aayi selflessly demolished her house and constructed a pond for the welfare of people. From that point on, the pond became known as Aayi Kulam.

When the French settled in Puducherry, they initiated various irrigation and drinking water projects across the region. The French Surveyors identified Aayi Kulam and found that the water is potable. Fascinated by the story, during the rule of Napoléon-III, the French, as a mark of respect towards Aayi, built a Memorial in the middle of Fort Louis. Situated in the middle of the Bharathi Park, this historical landmark is known as Aayi Mandapam.

The residents of Muthirapalayam fondly remember Aayi Kulam as a source of drinking water. However, over the years, due to neglect and encroachment, Aayi Kulam has shrunk into a small water body. The degradation of the water body began by the end of 2000, and the aggressive physical encroachments in and around the pond were left unattended. While the government had made attempts to rejuvenate the pond, the results were not significant. Nevertheless, a few voluntary organizations have been making efforts to revive the pond through Shramdaan. In 2018, Lt. Governor Dr. Kiran Bedi visited Aayi Kulam and discussed measures with the Municipal Administration and other officials. Since then, the administration has taken significant steps, desilting 178 ponds and cleaning up 720 KM of canals in Karaikal. Special importance was given to reviving every small water body, leading to their successful rejuvenation. The remarkable outcome of these efforts was seen when the water table rose by 10 ft within just 3 months. During my visit, I was astounded by the transformative work carried out by the Karaikal Collectorate in making Karaikal water-rich through creative, cost-effective, and collaborative efforts. The Namme Neer Programme played a vital role in this endeavor, as it integrated various stakeholders, including Public Sector Units and the local community, to rejuvenate numerous lost ponds and channels. The success of the Namme Neer Programme demonstrated the power of a collaborative approach involving multiple stakeholders, and it stands as a testament to the incredible work done to make Karaikal water-rich and sustainable.

My understanding of the Best Practices & Innovative Interventions in Karaikal involved the Namme Neer Programme - a mass movement advocating for rainwater conservation with the collaborative support of Government employees, non-governmental organizations, academics, experts, elected representatives, government departments, and the local community. The primary focus was to ensure that the program became a community-based activity encouraging active participation and ownership from the residents.

The conservation efforts were supplemented by IEC activities through awareness campaign activities by NSS, SHGs, Nehru Yuva Kendra, and social media, along with various line departments to promote efficient water use. Additionally, aquifers in ponds and water bodies that may have been encroached were also cleared during the Namme Neer programme. Gram Sabha meetings and Farmers Meets conducted by the district administration were used as platforms to disseminate the idea and gather collective inputs. All India Radio, print and television media, public functions, school and college events, and social media platforms such as the district Facebook page, WhatsApp groups, Twitter handles were effectively utilized to spread the message on multiple platforms across diverse segments. An integrated approach for participation of several stakeholders was undertaken during the course of the Namme Neer Programme. It involved tank de-siltation, restoration of the feeder channels, re-sectioning of irrigation channels, repairs to bunds, weirs, and sluices, and raising of FTL (Full Tank Level) to enhance water management and storage. The concept of Employee Social Responsibility opened the flood gates for the Namme Neer Programme, garnering significant support and participation.

An appeal was made to all Government Employees of Karaikal District to adopt a pond for rejuvenation. Taking the first step, officers and staff of the Collectorate adopted Vaathu Kulam at Keezhakasakudy Village. Subsequently, officers and staff working in various Government Departments in Karaikal district also adopted ponds in different communes of Karaikal under Employee Social Responsibility (ESR). This proactive approach provided the much-needed impetus for the programme, and various merchant communities, commercial establishments, and organizations followed suit, starting to adopt ponds for rejuvenation.

The District Administration sought to build and develop a funding and permitting framework to facilitate the voluntary adoption and rejuvenation of ponds and canals. The role of District Administration was limited to providing technical support and issue of No Objection | clearance with a pre-condition that de-silted sand should be used to construct the bunds and no sale of sand was allowed. Payments to contractor were directly made by the adopting agencies | departments | individuals | groups etc.

For the intense afforestation program, applicants of Cracker Sale Licenses were asked to plant a specific number of tree saplings in schools and colleges. Petrol Bunk owners were asked to plant trees in public spaces, parks, and beaches. Under ESR, departments were asked to plant trees alongside the ponds. Colleges with hostels and major restaurants have been addressed to use treated grey water to water crops. The possibility of deploying an automated drip fertigation system has also been insisted. The Namme Neer Karaikal initiative ensured an increase in the storage capacity of tanks and other water bodies. The district was ready to store 1 tmcft of water in all the ponds, including the rejuvenated Nallambal lake.

The Lieutenant Governor appreciated the efforts of the Collectorate and spoke about the need to sustain the desilted ponds through constant supervisions. At a recap session, the need for geo-tagging and ways to spread awareness were discussed in the meeting. The 236th Morning Round to Karaikal had further intensified Mission Water Rich and Green Puducherry initiative taken up by the Puducherry administration.

Quick Lunch at Karaikal on 2nd November 2019

Lt. Governor inspecting progress in the cleaning of polluted water body

MY KEY TAKEAWAYS FROM NAMME NEER KARAIKAL:

- Participatory approach can help in the judicious use of resources.

- Restoration and maintenance of water resources should be a continual process, and local people should be trained to manage them.

- Shifting from rain-dependent farming to harvesting and storing rainwater is crucial for efficient crop cultivation.

- Engaging communities in the implementation process reduces the need for government support, making the program self-reliant and socially sustainable.

- Improving on-farm moisture retention capacity leads to increased agricultural productivity.

- The initiative fosters the development of fisheries, livestock, and helps raise the groundwater level.

- The intense afforestation drive increases the green cover of Karaikal District and decreases the carbon footprint, aiding in combating climate change.

Creating awareness on Mission Water Rich Puducherry

Interns collaborate with student community for the afforestation programme

Chapter 7

SITHERI CHANNEL WALK

Channel Walk on the importance of rejuvenating water bodies

The Sitheri Channel Walk was a seven-kilometer walk as part of Mission Water Rich Puducherry. It required meticulous planning and resource mobilization to ensure a successful event for the Lieutenant Governor. The aim of the walk was to create awareness on protecting our natural resources for a sustainable future. I chalked out accurate details like the starting point and ending point of the walk, length of the walk and breakfast area which will be convenient for the team before submitting the relevant details to the Office of Lieutenant Governor. We left from Raj Nivas at 7:15 in the morning. Firstly, the Lieutenant Governor recognized the contributions of the donors and volunteers in clearing up the channel. I understood the importance of creating awareness for water conservation amongst the people.

Dr. Kiran Bedi, coined the word 'Weekend Water Walks'. I learnt the effects of desilting which is the removal of earthly materials such as sand and mud from the bed of fast flowing river. These earthly deposits over the time can lead to blockages which could cause obstructions to the free-flowing movement of water which could in turn lead to flooding. In rural areas we needed water in irrigation channels and in urban areas we needed to prevent the overflowing of the drains. The effect of desilting had encouraged the local community to be the real stakeholders and monitor the water bodies. Desilting had allowed the farmers to take the silt. The silt is rich in nutrients and the farmers are not charged for taking the silt. It helped the farmers in improving the yield in the next agricultural cycle. The desilting work had improved the ecology of the area and the groundwater aquifer was also protected. Desilting has helped the soil to be more fertile and the groundwater level had also been increasing due to the monsoon rain.

Local knowledge and traditional engineering played a crucial role in the successful desilting work. The presence of aqueducts significantly improved the flow rate of water, enhancing the overall efficiency of the water system. Desilting of rural canals not only improved water retention and carrying capacity but also facilitated the free flow of water, effectively preventing the spread of diseases like malaria and dengue.

This approach proved to be a win-win situation for the citizens, as it benefited the people by ensuring water availability and preventing water scarcity. The rejuvenation of the entire system through desilting had a positive impact on the residents, bringing them comfort and convenience. However, it was essential to raise awareness about the benefits and significance of desilting among the public, as many were unaware of its importance. Spreading knowledge about this practice would contribute to its wider adoption and further water conservation efforts.

During the channel walk, I had a chance to witness the tremendous efforts put in by the Public Works Department (PWD). It became evident that regular follow-ups and constant supervision were necessary to maintain the desilted channels effectively. The success of the Puducherry Model in making the region water-rich highlighted the need for conducting an impact assessment and comprehensive documentation of the project. The insights and learnings from this model could potentially be applied to make India water-rich as well. The field visit provided us, the interns, with a hands-on experience, offering a deeper understanding of the challenges and efforts involved in water conservation and rejuvenation initiatives. It was truly rewarding to be part of such a meaningful and impactful project.

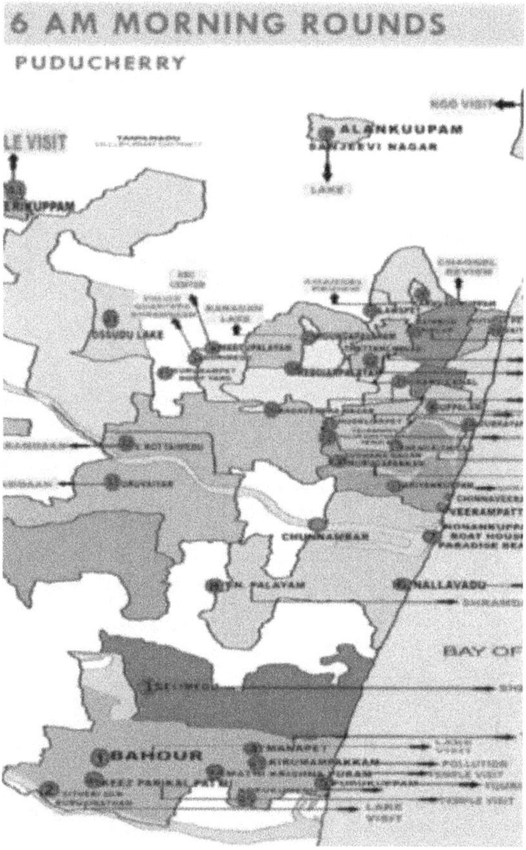

I had the opportunity to observe the review meetings conducted by Team Raj Nivas to assess the progress of various missions. One such meeting took place in the last week of October 2019 at the Durbar Hall of Raj Nivas. It was attended by the Chief Secretary and officials of the Puducherry Government. My responsibility during the meeting was to pass on the microphone to the Secretaries as required. The session continued until 9.30 PM, and after a quick dinner, I continued with further work until I reached my residence at 11.55 PM. Despite standing for nearly four hours, I fulfilled my duties diligently, which was acknowledged and appreciated by Lt. Governor Dr. Kiran Bedi. Travelling in the convoy of Lt. Governor for field visits and weekend rounds provided me with a surreal experience that we get to witness during the arrival of high-profile leaders telecasted in the news channels. The transparency, accessibility, and openness demonstrated by Dr. Kiran Bedi in her governance truly left a lasting impression on me. It was a remarkable experience to witness such a dedicated and dynamic leadership firsthand.

The Sitheri Channel Walk provided me with valuable lessons, including:

1. The significance of desilting in water conservation and utilization.

2. The importance of incorporating local knowledge and traditional engineering practices in such projects.

3. Understanding the role of aqueducts in facilitating a higher flow rate of water.

4. Recognizing how desilting efforts contribute to improving the ecology of the area.

Sitheri Channel Walk

I organized an educational tour for students from different schools with the aim to raise awareness about the need and benefits of desilting. It helped in motivating the youth to initiate a water conservation movement and pledge to save water.

AN EDUCATIONAL TOUR FOR STUDENTS FROM SITHERI ANICUT TO MANEPAT

1. **Aim of the Walk:**

    - Create awareness about the importance and benefits of desilting.

    - Motivate students to initiate a water conservation movement and commit to saving water.

2. **Salient Features:**

    - Paddy Field - Watering/Irrigation

    - Bridges, Culverts, and Streams

    - Uchhimedu Lake

    - Manepat Surplus

    - Manepat Lake

3. **Benefits of Desilting:**

    - Improves the ecology of the area.

    - Rejuvenates the entire biodiversity.

    - Increases the stability of groundwater levels.

    - Provides water to seven water tanks.

    - Surplus water rejuvenates the water table in the area.

4. **Benefits of the Channel Walk:**

    - The students should be able to see first-hand that Puducherry has an excellent irrigation system owing to its history of being wisely built during the times of the Cholas and the Pandavas. Farmers will be able to use surface and channel water instead of borewell.

SITHERI CHANNEL WALK

Penning down running notes during the Sitheri Channel Walk

Chapter 8

SMALL ACTS MAKE BIG IMPACTS

Morning walk at the Lawns of Raj Nivas

The title for this chapter would give the readers an insight into a short story that we don't get to read in our newspapers or watch on television channels. On the 19th of January 2020, I travelled to Raj Nivas for assisting Intern Snighdha from Harvard University in assessing the impact of Mission Water Rich Puducherry. My role involved communication and translation from Tamil to English. The 20th of January remains to be a remarkable learning experience. At Raj Nivas' lawns, an NGO group from Yanam were engaged in a discussion when Lt. Governor Dr. Kiran Bedi noticed a group of tourists waiting outside the gates. They hoped to catch a glimpse of the renowned leader and observe the palace environment. Acting promptly, Dr. Kiran Bedi instructed the guards to open the gate for the tourists. Among the visitors, a person introduced herself as a teacher from Uttar Pradesh. Overwhelmed with emotion, she shared that she taught the life of Dr. Kiran Bedi, India's most admired police officer, to her students. The "Top-Cop" was a beloved figure to the children, who eagerly listened to anecdotes about her. Before departing, the tourists gratefully took a group photo with the Lt. Governor. This encounter left a lasting impression on me, teaching an important lesson: true leadership lies in the actions that may go unnoticed by the world at large but has a profound impact on the lives of individuals and small groups. The teacher from Uttar Pradesh will forever cherish this unforgettable moment in her life, showing that the influence of a leader can touch hearts across distances and leave an indelible mark on those they inspire.

I vividly remember a memorable walk with Dr. Kiran Bedi before the arrival of the NGO group at Raj Nivas. Lt.Governor asked me to stroll around the scenic lush green lawns of the palace, and as we walked, madam inquired about the data collected from the field study to assess the impact of Mission Water Rich Puducherry. The assessment pattern designed by Snigdha from Harvard University included several metrics:

1. Uses of water from tanks (cattle, domestic use, drinking, agriculture use)

2. Rise in land value – timeline trend.

3. Did the total annual income change after desilting?

4. Fetching water – what was it like before, and what is the situation now?

5. Flooding of fields – before desilting and after desilting?

6. Any effect on livestock?

7. How is a change in crop yield measured?

I explained these metrics, and the reply we received from the farming community included a message of gratitude to the Lt. Governor. One farmer had a suggestion for the desilted sites to ensure longevity in the work. As I conveyed the request, a quick and firm reply came from Dr. Kiran Bedi that it would be immediately granted, and necessary changes would be adopted to enhance the productivity of the work executed for the welfare of the farming community. India's renowned police officer and first citizen of a Union Territory listening to an ordinary law student and ensuring that such field reports are recognized and immediately implemented speak volumes about the leader within Dr. Kiran Bedi. This incident reminded me of a story that Mahatma Gandhi's mother told to the then-school-going Mohandas Karamchand Gandhi – that if he could help one person around him in his life, it would be a true mark of leading a successful life.

Following the footsteps of Mahatma Gandhi and Dr. Kiran Bedi, let us all be inspired!

Chapter 9

OUTREACH PROGRAMMES

Education lies at the heart of every society's future; it is the central component for the progress of a nation. Educational improvements are directly proportional to the well-being, economic development, quality of life, and overall development of a country. The outreach programmes by Team Raj Nivas became a pivotal project as part of good governance. These programmes included reaching out to Government schools across different areas in Puducherry.

Distributing stationary@TN Palayam Govt Middle School

Addressing the children @TN Palayam Govt Middle School

I extensively prepared plenty of activities for the children. Few of them included:

1. Find out the leaders - This activity featured pictures of great Indian leaders such as Mahatma Gandhi, Netaji Subhash Chandra Bose, and Pandit Jawaharlal Nehru. The children participated in a competition to answer questions related to these leaders.

2. Other activities included discussing the environmental importance and its correlation with Mission Green Puducherry and Mission Water Rich Puducherry. The children actively shared their thoughts and ideas on protecting the environment.

Preparing to ask the quiz questions

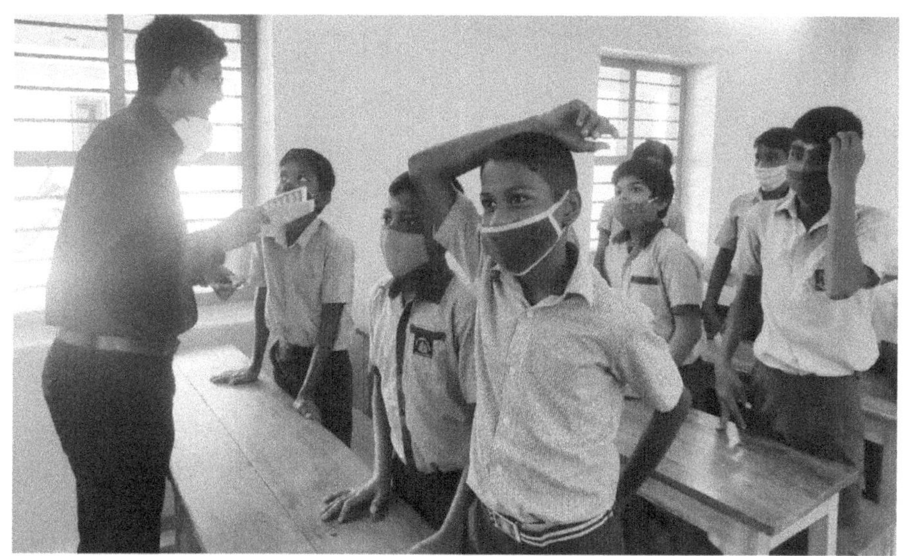

Teaching Self – Affirmation Mantras

I gave them the following Mantra- "Yes, I Can" as part of the self-affirmations essential to a child's progress. Lt. Governor Dr. Kiran Bedi adopted schools which lacked necessities such as pencils and other stationary requirements. We collected a certain sum to provide the school children with color pencils, crayons, shoes, and toys. The principal noted that before the adoption by Dr. Kiran Bedi, it was more of a school lacking teaching materials for imparting quality education. It is now a story of the "past." The outreach programs created an impact on the students.

- **Physically** – Concentrating on food, play, sleep, etc.

- **Emotionally** – facing all challenges in life with the utmost confidence and determination.

- **Socially** – developing a strong personality where they will live a fulfilled life. Utmost care in character-building, such as discipline, respecting individual opinions, working on problem-solving through teamwork and perseverance, was emphasized by the Lt. Governor.

- **Intellectual Development** – Lt. Governor Dr. Kiran Bedi asked students to enrich their knowledge to adapt to the transformative needs of society.

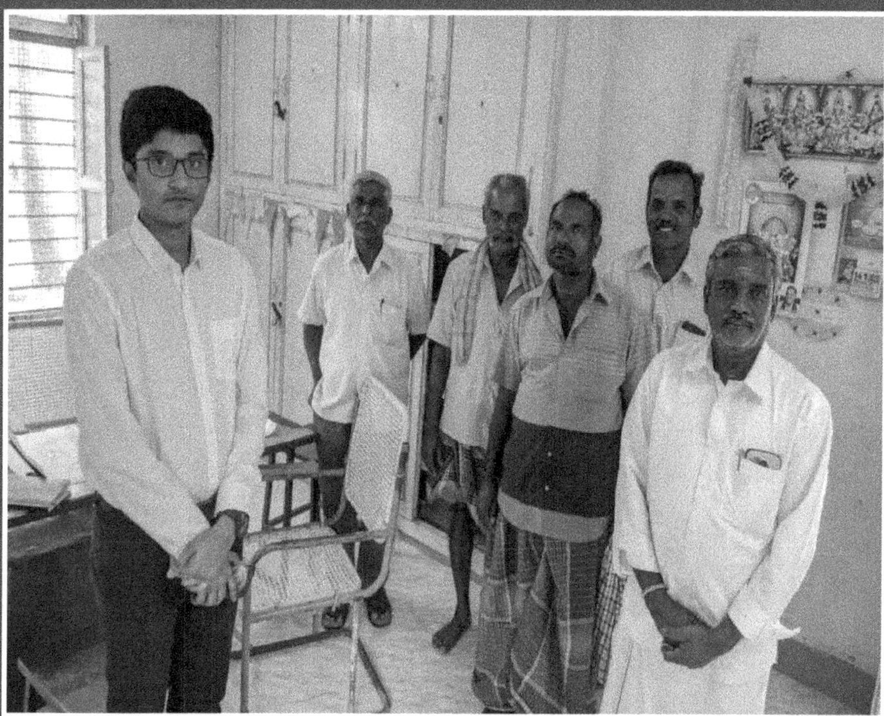

Discussion on Water Rich Puducherry with the farming community

Interns meeting aftermath the Covid first wave

Few other Outreach Programmes which I led were:

- **"Film Series"** – A series of movies telecasted at Raj Nivas to motivate the children and allow them to spend an evening surrounded by the green lawns of the Governor's palace received a lightning response from the school community. Every inch of the available space was occupied during the evening at Raj Nivas. After the movie, I guided the children around Raj Nivas. They were allowed to see the historical Durbar Hall and ancient artifacts.

- **Visitor's Hour** – Residents of Puducherry and tourists from across the nation had a glimpse of the splendid home and office of Dr. Kiran Bedi in the seat of constitutional power. They were permitted to take pictures for everlasting memories. Visitor's Hour opened the Governor's palace to the common people. This was a golden period that saw the opening of the Governor's office with accessibility, unlike the numerous 'closed gates' we find across the nation. A lesson to all the 'Public Servants' that accessibility and open offices for citizens are essential duties in the line of service.

- **Cycle Rallies** – I understood the impact of Cycle rallies in creating an eye-catching awareness with the participation of NGOs, students, and volunteers spearheading rallies to sensitize people on road safety, environmental protection, women empowerment, etc. The Lt. Governor's participation boosted the confidence of participants intending to create an impact on our society.

Cycling at Auroville Forest - February 2021

Cycling with Team Raj Nivas and Interns

Completing the Weekend Round at Auroville Forest

Chapter 10

BOOK RELEASE AND REPUBLIC DAY 2020

Meeting Dr. Karan Singh after the book release in Puducherry

Dr. Karan Singh's illustrious career came to the highlight as the book "Reflections" – Anthology of Essays" was released by Dr. Kiran Bedi. A serene evening on the eve of Republic Day in Puducherry. I read an exciting chapter in the book titled "India: A Future World Power" which describes the heroics of the Indian past. The unparalleled legacy of diverse kingdoms and rulers of Pre-Independent India came to the spotlight as Dr. Karan Singh told the multitude of experiences from being the regent of the Princely State of Jammu and Kashmir to the first Sadr-e-Riyasat to India's youngest serving Cabinet Minister marked the life of a scholar with rich knowledge of the ancient scriptures as well as the modern world that has seen a technological revolution. The event began with welcome messages and bouquets of gratitude as part of the formal acknowledgements.

The crucial lessons that I learnt from this book are the four pillars of excellence described by Dr. Karan Singh, which are:

1. Learning to Know
2. Learning to Do
3. Learning to Live Together
4. Learning to be a Worldly Citizen

Interns pose for a group picture with Lt. Governor Dr. Kiran Bedi, Dr. Karan Singh and Comptroller Mrs. Asha Gupta.

Asking a question to Dr. Karan Singh on his illustrious career

Dr. Karan Singh described the times when Independent India's First Prime Minister Pandit Jawaharlal Nehru visited the Royal Family in Jammu and Kashmir as part of the historical shift in the independence and administration of the State. Mahatma Gandhi and distinguished freedom fighters marked their presence in cooperation with Maharaja Hari Singh as the State acceded to the Indian Union. It was an hour of re-living impactful moments, such as the changes in geographical landscape leading to the formation of Bangladesh as an independent nation. Dr. Karan Singh vividly recalled his brief tenure as the Indian Ambassador to the United States of America, which had given him a remarkable learning experience in his journey of Public Service.

Interns were permitted to ask questions after the book release, with Lt. Governor Dr. Kiran Bedi asking us to fully utilize this opportunity as we conversed with Dr. Karan Singh. My question on moments of eternal joy received a spiritually charged answer from Dr. Karan Singh, mentioning that Dance of Shiva by Yamini Krishnamurti transports him to a different world and gives a tremendous boost in his life. The book release came to a fruitful conclusion as I prepared to attend and participate in the nation's 71st Republic Day.

The Republic Day - 2020 was an occasion for the interns to gather together in celebrating the day by singing patriotic songs and attending the Republic Day Parade at Indira Gandhi Sports Complex, Uppalam, Puducherry. We were seated in the space reserved for the family of Lt. Governor Dr. Kiran Bedi. Unfurling the National Flag and witnessing enthralling performances marked a memorable day in my internship experience. We gathered in the evening of 26th January 2020 to share our progress in the dining hall of Raj Nivas. Dr. Kiran Bedi remarked the following – "Children, I have given you all everything in my powers and I pray to God for strength, so that I can do more for you all". As the ivory gates were opened up for the people, ma'am greeted the visitors from balcony and asked the interns to stand beside and greet the citizens. Ordinary students were made to feel extraordinary by Lieutenant Governor Dr. Kiran Bedi. I prepared to work at Raj Nivas during the summer vacation unaware of the waiting global pandemic.

Eve of Republic Day with Lt. Governor Dr. Kiran Bedi and Interns

Raj Nivas glows in the background with patriotic colours

Republic Day Parade - 2020

Left to Right: Officer on Special Duty Shri G Theva Neethi Dhas, Intern Karthik, Chief Secretary Mr. Ashwani Kumar, Myself and Intern Sabari

Chapter 11

ONLINE DURING COVID

The Covid Pandemic posed a challenge in administrative work, requiring innovative and creative approaches in dealing with the global pandemic. Lt. Governor devised a systematic method to virtually create platforms such as:

- Virtual Open House
- Virtual Celebration of Festivals
- Virtual Internship, thereby ensuring continuity in the work executed by Team Raj Nivas. I had the following tasks as an online intern -

1. Prepare Research Papers.
2. Creation and compilation of videos along with subtitles.
3. Collaboration and Documentation of various Newspaper Clips.

I had the opportunity to work on various tasks as an online intern during the pandemic, which allowed me to enhance my skills despite the disruptions in traditional education. I am attaching below few of the diverse collaboration of news articles as a glimpse into the world of my online work:

Lockdown rules, Section 144 should be strictly observed: Kiran Bedi

Free Rice Distribution To 60% Beneficiaries Completed in Puducherry: Kiran Bedi

The lockdown was first announced by Prime Minister Narendra Modi on March 24 in a bid to combat the Coronavirus endemic. It was further extended till May 3.

All India Press Trust of India Updated: April 26, 2020

11:44 am IST *by Taboola*

Puducherry was the first to start MGNREGA work after centre relaxed lockdown guidelines, she said

PUDUCHERRY: The Puducherry administration has distributed free rice to over 60% of beneficiaries under the Pradhan Mantri Garib Kalyan Ann Yojana to mitigate their sufferings and hardships due to the nationwide lockdown to combat the novel coronavirus, Lieutenant Governor Kiran Bedi has said. Talking to PTI over the phone, she said, "I sincerely thank Prime Minister Narendra Modi and the central government for helping the UT (Union Territory) administration to provide free rice for three months to 6.5 lakh poor and downtrodden beneficiaries to mitigate their hardship due to the COVID-19 lockdown. Rice has already been distributed to over 60% of the beneficiaries under the Pradhan Mantri Garib Kalyan Ann Yojana. The UT government lifted 9,425 tonnes of additional rice from FCI (Food Corporation of India) and has already distributed over 6,000 tonnes," she said.

Similarly, the Centre has increased the daily wage to labourers under the Mahatma Gandhi National Rural Employment Guarantee Act (MGNREGA) to ₹259 from ₹229, with effect from this month. Puducherry is the first government in the country to start MGNREGA work after the Union Home Ministry relaxed lockdown guidelines from April 20, she said. Likewise, the Centre has credited ₹500 each to the bank accounts of 83,000 women beneficiaries in the first week of this month under the Pradhan Mantri Jan Dhan Yojana, the former IPS officer said, adding that a whopping ₹4.15 crore has reached the women beneficiaries in Puducherry. The Ramon Magsaysay awardee of 1994 said 9,299 farmers of the UT have already received the first installment of ₹2,000 each (out of ₹6,000 per year) under the PM Kisan Samman Nidhi Yojana. Under the scheme, aimed at helping small and medium farmers, ₹1,85,98,000 has been released for 2020-21.

"Remaining 913 farmers will receive the benefit by direct bank transfer shortly as the process is already on," she said.

Kiran Bedi asks people to share info on illegal liquor sale in Puducherry

TNN | May 6, 2020, 09.02 PM IST

PUDUCHERRY: Puducherry Lieutenant Governor Kiran Bedi on Wednesday appealed to people in the Union Territory to share information on the illegal sale of liquor during the lockdown period with the CBI. They can also share information with Raj Nivas Chief Grievances Officer S Bascarane on WhatsApp (95005 60001). Bedi said the CBI has commenced an investigation into the illegal sale of liquor during the lockdown period by unknown people in connivance with unknown government officials. She said police have suspended the licenses of 100 shops selling Indian-made foreign liquor, arrack, toddy and registered 236 cases. Police arrested eight government servants and transferred a few for their involvement in the illegal activity. The Deputy Commissioner of Excise was removed to ensure a fair investigation, she said.

Posted at: Jul 1 2020 11:55AM

Pondy LG Greets Doctors on National Doctors day

Puducherry, Jul 1 (UNI) Lt.Governor Kiran Bedi greeted the doctors community on behalf of the people of Puducherry and on behalf of the Raj Nivas on 'National Doctors Day" on Wednesday.

In a whatsapp posting, she thanked all the doctors who are saving the lives in Puducherry and around the country.

"We cannot thank them enough for the lives they are saving. They are serving in very very harsh conditions and yet they continue to work for hours together', Ms Bedi added.

Please log in to get detailed story.

PUDUCHERRY, JULY 08, 2020 14:53 IST

Lt. Governor Kiran Bedi on Sunday asked the people of Puducherry to be very cautious till the COVID-19 situation in neighbouring Tamil Nadu returned to normalcy. In a video message, Ms. Bedi said an improvement of the situation in Puducherry in large part depended on how the pandemic was playing out in the neighbouring districts, as well as Chennai, because of the interconnectedness of these places.

Many people from neighbouring districts may have entered Puducherry without knowing that they had been infected, Ms. Bedi said. This is not the time for visits, but the time to exercise utmost care and care to prevent spread of the COVID-19, especially as cases have been increasing at worrying levels in recent weeks in Puducherry, Ms. Bedi said

Kiran Bedi appeals to elected representatives

Lt. Governor Kiran Bedi on Sunday appealed to elected representatives to set an example in the adoption of COVID-19 safety norms.

Pointing to a few photographs and reports in the media showing violation of social distancing norms by public figures, Ms. Bedi said this happened after some people's representatives had tested positive. Unless the political leadership show respect for whatever they want the public to do, the war against COVID-19 would be a case of taking two steps forward and three steps backwards, she added.

"It is the need of the hour that every single public representative takes responsibility for his own area and observes personal discipline," she said.

Bring All Private Medical College on Board for COVID Treatment: Kiran Bedi Asks PM Modi, Home Minister – Medical Dialogues:

PUDUCHERRY: The Union health and family welfare ministry has deputed a central team to Puducherry to assist it in the clinical management of Covid-19 infection following a plea made by Lieutenant Governor Kiran Bedi.

Rise in Covid-19 cases in India due to flouting of norms by people: Kiran Bedi

Puducherry Lieutenant Governor Kiran Bedi has attributed the spurt in coronavirus cases in India to the violation of safety protocols such as social distancing by the public. Expressing strong concern over the flouting of norms by the people, Bedi, in a video message on Saturday, said, "With the people violating relevant safety protocols such as social distancing, there has been a huge spike in pandemic cases in India."

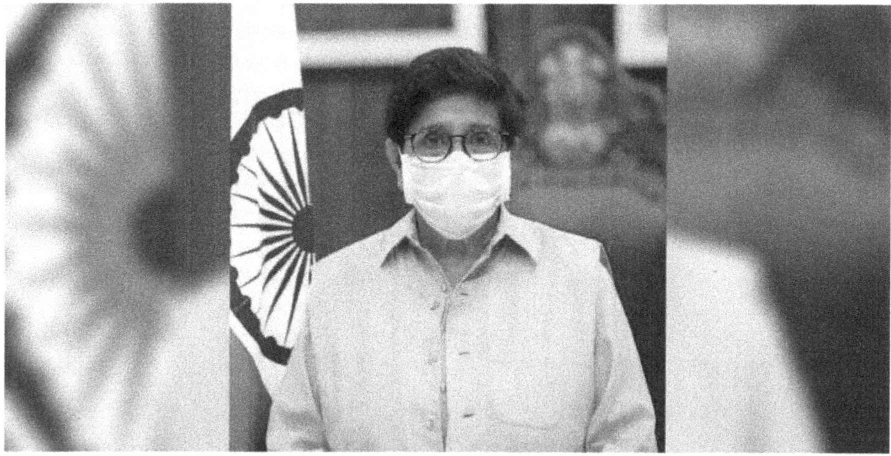

In a veiled reference to the breach of rules by people in Puducherry, she said when the lockdown was lifted, there were serpentine queues outside liquor shops, and people were seen jostling with each other to purchase alcohol. Similarly, during the Vinayaka Chaturthi celebrations, people were seen moving about in the open, and there were processions carried out despite the appeal made to celebrate the festival at home. Bedi expressed regret that some people expect the government to provide treatment free of cost after violating the safety norms and causing the spread of the virus. She sought to know why everything should come from the government and why not the people pay for the services.

Puducherry Lt Governor Kiran Bedi appoints top IAS officer to check Covid-19 situation

Senior IAS officer and UT development commissioner, A. Anbarasu has been appointed as the relief and Rehabilitation Commissioner to monitor and manage the pandemic situation.

- *ETGovernment*

- On September 03, 2020, at 10:11 AM IST, the Lt. Governor of Puducherry, Kiran Bedi, took action to address the increase in Covid-19 cases in the region. She appointed senior IAS officer and UT development commissioner, A Anbarasu, as the Relief and Rehabilitation Commissioner. Anbarasu's new role aims to enhance oversight and coordination among all departments and private medical colleges to control the rise in Covid-19 cases. The government's objective is to improve communication with the public and provide reassurance during this pandemic situation.

According to the chief secretary Ashwani Kumari, the orders issued by the Lt Governor's office have come into immediate effect. As per the role assigned to Anbarasu, he will work closely with the teams deputed by the Centre to Puducherry in the context of evolving measures to battle the pandemic. He will also review and mobilise more resources to lead the strategies already proposed by the teams from JIPMER and ICMR to tackle the situation. Meanwhile, Lt Governor Kiran Bedi has also asked the Relief and Rehabilitation Commission to work together with the Puducherry government and the Central teams "to win over the people's confidence as the next two to three weeks will be critical," the government note said.

Chapter 12

LEGAL LEARNINGS

10 AM Meeting @office of Lt. Governor Dr. Kiran Bedi

One of the essential subjects in the field of law is "Constitutional Law," with its complete understanding necessary for a law student. The powers possessed by the President of India, Vice–President of India, Prime Minister of India, Council of Ministers, Judges, Governors, Lt. Governors, and other public offices are key to this subject. Understanding the separation of powers between the legislature, executive, and judiciary is a student's fundamental learning. As an intern at Raj Nivas, I had the following legal understandings:

A. Experiencing the life and powers of a Lt. Governor helped me to differentiate the powers held by Governors and Lt. Governors of a Union Territory. This practical experience made a vast difference compared to theoretical learning in a classroom. The significant difference is that positions of power can foster development and ensure administrative justice. Lt. Governor Dr. Kiran Bedi ensured that the position of a Lt. Governor is used to the fullest extent to increase the quality of life for the citizens of Puducherry.

B. The legislative assembly of Puducherry is unique in its identity, with thirty elected members and three members nominated by the Lt. Governor. As interns, we closely witnessed the functioning of the political executive headed by the Chief Minister and Cabinet.

C. As part of Mission Water Rich Puducherry and Green Puducherry, interns worked with the Collector, Tahsildar, and officials with the Public Works Department. Observing the functioning of the Police Department and Bureaucracy gave an insightful analysis of the Government structure laid down by the Indian Constitution.

D. Field visits and Weekend Rounds to Police Stations as part of inspections played a role in strengthening the beat policing system. Interns understood the crucial role played by the Police in upholding law and order as well as preventing and detecting crime.

E. The role of Lok Adalats in the Grievance Redressal System gave us an important understanding of the Alternative Dispute Mechanisms. It works to reduce the large number of cases pending in the Indian Judiciary by a process of mutual settlement.

F. The Madras High Court upheld the contentions of the Lt. Governor possessing more expansive administrative powers in a series of petitions filed by the political executive. My first visit to a court remains to be the Madras High Court's Chief Justice Courtroom to hear the arguments between the counsels. At the request of both parties, the arguments were posted after a month by the Court.

Museum at Madras High Court

After the visit to Madras High Court, I met Senior Advocate Shri. Aman Lekhi representing Lt. Governor. Fortunately, it led to my legal internship in New Delhi. My Internship at Raj Nivas laid the foundation for a fruitful learning experience in New Delhi.

Meeting with Additional Solicitor General of India Shri Aman Lekhi

AMAN LEKHI
ADDITIONAL SOLICITOR GENERAL OF INDIA

TO WHOMSOEVER IT MAY CONCERN

This is to certify that K. Krithik Kailash, third year student of B.A.LLB. [Hons.] at Christ University, Bangalore has successfully completed his internship under my guidance from 4th October to 28th October 2021.

During his Internship, Krithik has worked on matters pertaining to Prevention of Corruption Act, Prevention of Money Laundering Act, Armed Forces Tribunal Act, NDPS Act, Indian Evidence Act, Code of Criminal Procedure and Indian Penal Code. He has assisted in drafting of opinions and preparing notes on briefs for matters. Under the guidance of the associates, he has actively involved himself in research and attended virtual hearing before the Supreme Court and various High Courts regularly across India.

During my interaction with him, I found Krithik to be diligent, competent, and sincere. He is receptive to new ideas, concepts and displays keen eagerness to learn. Krithik also took initiative in discussion in office, demonstrated good understanding of law and possess strong analytical skills.

I wish him all the success in future endeavors.

Aman Lekhi:

28.10.2021

SE-122, Law Officers' Chambers, Supreme Court of India, New Delhi-110001. Phone : 91-11-23074158
C-98A, New Delhi South Extension Part II, New Delhi-110049. Phones : 91-11-26251814, 26252283
e-mail : office@amanlekhi.com

1940. Judges Of Madras High Court

A Galaxy of Erudite Judges

The Madras High Court is credited with an enviable reputation for the quality of its Bench and Bar. For the first time in Madras Presidency, an Indian was appointed as a judge of the Madras High Court as early as in 1877. That was Justice Sir T. Muthusamy Iyer, who rose to the enviable position of a judge of the High Court from the humble post of Munsiff and ultimately, the Acting Chief Justice of the Madras High Court in 1893.

Sir T. Muthusamy Iyer

Sir V. Bhashyam Aiyangar

The British Government appointed Sir V. Bhashyam Aiyangar, a distinguished Vakil of the Madras High Court, as the (First Indian) Acting Advocate General – February 1897 – March 1898 and September 1899 – March 1900. In 1901, he was elevated as Judge of this Court. He drafted the Madras General Clauses Act in 1891 and the same was adopted as General Clauses Act in 1897. The rich body of case laws that developed under this statute guides interpretation of statutes till this date.

Dr. P. V. Rajamannar was the first Indian to become Chief Justice of Madras High Court after independence (1948-1961) and he served as Chief Justice for 13 long years.

Other notables include Justices. K.Sundaram Chetty, P.R.Sundara Iyer, Sir C.V.Kumaraswami Sastriar, Sir Vepa Ramesam, Muthiah David Devadon, Sir Muthu Venka Subba Rao, Rao Bhadur Dr.K.K.Pandalay, Justice Dr.P.Venkatramana Rao, Justice K.Subba Rao, Justice A.V.Viswanatha Sastri and Justice Basheer Ahmed Sayeed. This list is by no means exhaustive but merely indicative of the rich judicial talent that adorned benches of the Madras High Court.

Dr. P. V. Rajamannar

A Picture from the Museum at Madras High Court

Chapter 13

HISTORICAL DAYS

Presentation on the Kanagan Lake as part of Intern Lecture Series

As the pandemic's first wave came to an end, I returned to Raj Nivas for documenting the monumental efforts undertaken to clean Kanagan Lake. The Kanagan Lake is one of the oldest freshwater lakes situated in the region of Puducherry. It was a main source of irrigation in Reddiyarpalayam and Ulavarkalai. The lake which was once the main source of water for the residents came to a stage of extinction due to the neglection and contamination of the water. The process of urbanization reduced the lake to a small area of water body. In the year 2017, the despicable condition of the lake was brought to the notice of Lt. Governor Dr. Kiran Bedi. The lake was choked with water hyacinth and was receiving sewage water from the neighbourhood despite having sewage treatment plant in the nearby Medical College that was dysfunctional. The Government Departments, NSS Volunteers and students from various colleges collaborated to work together in reviving the lake. The scientific approach combined with the indomitable spirit of the people resulted in the restoration of Kanagan lake in a record two years of time.

The Lt. Governor regularly visited the site to guide the team towards completing the work. Review meetings were conducted after every visit to assess the progress of work on the ground. The cleaning of Kanagan Lake saw the rejuvenation of clear flowing water. More than 4 tons of water hyacinth were removed from the lake. Today, this is one of the most important water bodies in Puducherry. There was an unspeakable joy amongst the people in completing the mission to restore Kanagan Lake as part of Mission Green and Water Rich Puducherry. The lake has a pathway and is ring-fenced with trees that were planted by the volunteers to increase the beauty of the landscape. Community events like chanting of the Bhagavad Gita and playing sports like cricket brought the citizens together as one family, turning Mission Green and Water Rich Puducherry into a success story. Fishing has also become a daily routine in the lake. The sight of children gleefully playing as the sun sets is a scene that highlights the importance of guarding our environment for the welfare of people. It is indeed a story of challenges to protect and conserve Mother Nature's divine beauty, which is sacrosanct to the existence of life on Planet Earth.

TIMELINE OF EVENTS:

- 18 | 09 | 2016 - First visit to Kanagan Lake by Lt. Governor
- 10 | 09 | 2017 - 104th Weekend Round to Kanagan Lake.
- 30 | 12 | 2017 – Bicycle to Kanagan Lake by Lt. Governor Dr. Kiran Bedi.
- 13 | 01 | 2018 - 131st Weekend Round to Kanagan Lake to review the progress.
- 06 | 01 | 2018 - 133rd Weekend Round visit to Kanagan Lake.
- 20 | 10 | 2018 - 134th Weekend Round to Kanagan Lake by bicycle to review the work.
- 20 | 11 | 2018 - A video of restoration in Kanagan Lake posted on social media by Lieutenant Governor Dr. Kiran Bedi to create awareness of the ongoing efforts to clean the lake.
- 20 | 11 | 2018 - The revival of Kanagan Lake after several weekend visits brought substantial improvements in the water body.
- 27 | 01 | 2018 - 136th Weekend Round visit to Kanagan Lake. Plans for a walkway, planting of saplings, paddle and rowing boats for people to enjoy walking around the lake were decided.
- 31 | 02 | 2018 - Weekend Round 138 - By Bicycle
- 12 | 05 | 2019 - Interns at Raj Nivas clean the Kanagan Lake
- 09 | 06 | 2019 - 219th Weekend Round to Kanagan Lake.
- 23 | 06 | 2019 - Weekend Round - Tree plantation program
- 04 | 07 | 2019 - Geeta Chanting at Kanagan Lake by students of Vidyaniketan School.
- 24 | 06 | 2019 - The Lake was adopted by 2000 Students.
- 26 | 06 | 2019 - College students adopt the water body - to be maintained by them hereafter.
- 24 | 07 | 2019 - Pelicans sighted for the first time at Kanagan Lake;
- 04 | 11 | 2019 - Swachhata Hi Seva Award presented by Lt. Governor Dr. Kiran Bedi to the participants.
- 09 | 02 | 2020 - 253rd Weekend Round - Celebrating the Clean Kanagan Lake maintained by Resident Welfare Association of the area, co-opting with all agencies of the Government and Volunteers.
- 09 | 02 | 2020 - Attending the Heritage Festival on Water Bodies.

Lt. Governor Dr. Kiran Bedi reviews the cleaning of Kanagan Lake

LESSONS LEARNT:

1. **Field Visits**: The restoration of the Kanagan lake highlights the importance of field visits that were integral in cleaning the lake.

2. **Community Participation**: The community's active involvement ensured that the people became protectors of the lake, fostering sustainable community revitalization.

3. **Teamwork**: The cleaning of the lake saw the collaboration of various departments of Team Puducherry. The NSS Volunteers and students from various colleges worked together in reviving the lake.

4. **Leadership**: The leadership of Lt. Governor created further leaders in departments and communities, encouraging collective responsibility.

5. **Perseverance**: The consistent efforts of the people led to overcoming various challenges in cleaning the lake.

6. **Creative Thinking**: The scientific approach combined with practical ideas during the lake's cleaning was fundamental in achieving the goal.

7. **Visibility**: The cleaning of Kanagan Lake forged a team of volunteers, creating an impact on the community to voluntarily participate in reviving lakes and ponds.

8. **Documentation**: The documentation of the work done on Kanagan Lake reflects the importance of keeping a record to inspire and be a role model for emulation.

1. Field Visits:
The restoration of the Kanagan lake highlights the importance of field visits that were integral in cleaning the lake.

2. Community Participation:
The community participation has ensured that the people are the protectors of the lake. Only this can sustain community revitalization.

3. Teamwork:
The cleaning of the lake saw the collaboration of various departments of Team Puducherry. The NSS Volunteers and students from various colleges, worked together in reviving the lake.

4. Leadership:
The leadership of Lt. Governor Dr. Kiran Bedi was the mainreason for the revitalization of Kanagan Lake. This leadership created further leaders in departments, communities to take on collective responsibility.

Lessons Learnt:

5. Perseverance:
The consistent effort of the people in overcoming the challenges.

6. Creative Thinking:
The scientific approach combined with practical ideas during the cleaning of lake was fundamental in achieving the goal.

7. Visibility:
The cleaning of Kanagan Lake forged a team of volunteers which created an impact on the community to voluntarily participate in reviving lakes and ponds

8. Documentation:
The documentation of the work done on Kanagan Lake reflects the importance of keeping a record that will inspire the coming generations.

A graphical presentation for the lecture series

Removing the pollutants from the lake

Clear view of Kanakan Lake

TWEETS BY LT. GOVERNOR DR. KIRAN BEDI:

Kiran Bedi
@thekiranbedi

This morning visit shall lead to recovery of Kanagan Lake.
Shall visit this again next weekends till all decisions taken on the spot
and commitments made by the departments present are implemented.
This shall be r New Year Gift to people of Puducherry @rashtrapatibhvn
@PMOIndia

Kiran Bedi
@thekiranbedi

Meeting with CE and SE+ of PWD. Made them realise that Keeping
Puducherry #WaterRich/ #GreenPuducherry are their sacred duties.
Water bodies have to be filled up with maximum community
participation and support so that public money is invested where its
most essential & needed.

Presenting Survey Documents to the President of Resident Welfare Association Mr. Purushottam

Comptroller Mrs. Asha Gupta speaks on the progress of work to Lt. Governor

Documenting Green Puducherry with Team Raj Nivas

Mother Mrs. Arthy Lakshmi with Dr. Kiran Bedi for the Award Ceremony@Raj Nivas

Group picture at Auroville Forest – 2021

Group Picture with Comptroller Mrs. Asha Gupta and Team Raj Nivas as part of Mission Green Puducherry.

Field Work

NEWS ARTICLES:

Raj Nivas a mere facilitator in waterbodies' rejuvenation: Bedi

L-G fetes donors, leaders who helped in cleaning up ponds, drains and canals

SPECIAL CORRESPONDENT
PUDUCHERRY

The Raj Nivas only remained a "facilitator" in the drive to rejuvenate waterbodies under the corporate social responsibility programme, Lieutenant Governor Kiran Bedi said here on Monday.

Speaking at a function to felicitate donors and leaders who helped in reviving the ponds, canals and channels, the Lieutenant Governor said donors paid money directly to the contractor who is executing the programme.

Tracing the idea behind roping in donors for dredging the drinking and irrigation water sources in Puducherry and Karaikal regions, Ms. Bedi said during a weekend visit to Sitheri canal, a general discussion on dredging the fresh water sources emerged.

Officials who accompanied the Raj Nivas team, Ms. Bedi said, spoke about funds shortage to carry out the work. The contractors who desilted the canals in the past were yet to be paid, she said.

"We then enquired with a firm which benefited from the Sitheri canal as to whether it was interested to partner in the desilting process. From there on, we never looked back. It is only bet-

Recognising excellence: Lieutenant Governor Kiran Bedi handing over the 'Swachhata Awards 2019' to Puducherry Collector T. Arun at Raj Nivas ion Monday. Also seen are (from right) Karaikal Collector A. Vikranth Raja, Chief Secretary Ashwani Kumar and Regional Director (Southern Region) of Ministry of Corporate Affairs M.R. Bhat. •S.S. KUMAR

ween the giver and contractor," Ms. Bedi said.

The Lieutenant Governor praised the work of Puducherry District Collector T. Arun and Karaikal Collector Vikram Raja in implementing the programme.

Chief Secretary's appeal

Chief Secretary Ashwani Kumar said it was not necessary that the government should directly get involved in such endeavours.

Indirectly referring to the objections raised by certain quarters on the model adopted, Mr. Kumar said "when something good is happening allow it to happen."

There was delay in preparation of estimate and in execution, he said. "I am not saying the officials deliberately over-estimate the work. It is that the wheels are rather circuitous," he added.

The Chief Secretary appealed to the donors to adopt the waterbodies on which they had spent money for future maintenance. Mr. Arun said the district administration had identified 694 waterbodies in the region. Of these, 150 ponds were desilted under the CSR programme.

Also, 203 km of canals have been cleaned up under MGNREGA programme, he added.

His counterpart in Karaikal, Mr. Raja said the de-silting and rejuvenation of waterbodies had helped raise the water table by around 10 feet.

Raj Nivas honoured donors, distributed certificates to officials who led the team and multi-tasking staff of Public Works Department.

M.R. Bhat, Regional Director (Southern), Ministry of Corporate Affairs, and Theva Neethi Dhas, Officer on Special Duty, were present.

05 NOV 2019

Lieutenant Governor Kiran Bedi cingerisng Perumalpet lake on a bicycle on Sunday. | Campus

THE HINDU

1 0 JUN 2018

Will make Puducherry an ideal destination: Kiran Bedi

L-G celebrates her birthday with members of the public

SPECIAL CORRESPONDENT
PUDUCHERRY

The Raj Nivas was thrown open to the public on Saturday on the occasion of Lieutenant Governor Kiran Bedi's 69th birthday.

Ms. Bedi cut a cake in the presence of senior officials such as Chief Secretary Ashwani Kumar, Director General of Police S.K. Gautam, and officials of the Raj Nivas. Ms. Bedi was greeted by the public from 8 a.m. to 9 a.m. People from all walks of life, including former elected representatives, retired officers, and schoolchildren greeted her.

Chief Minister V. Narayanasamy, Speaker V. Vaithilingam and Ministers A. Na-

Lieutenant Governor Kiran Bedi cutting her birthday cake on Saturday. • S.S. KUMAR

massivayam, M. Kandasamy and M.O.H.F. Shahjahan greeted her on the occasion. AINRC chief N. Rangasamy too called on her.

Ms. Bedi told reporters that she found Puducherry a fantastic place to achieve everything easily and said that it was her commitment, along with that of officials, to make Puducherry prosperous. "I have enjoyed the trust and energy of the people. I would like to give back to the people of Puducherry the maximum," she added.

Karaikal visit

Later, the Lt. Governor left for Karaikal for the interaction with farmers and parents-teachers' association on women's security through responsible parenting of boys.

District Collector Satyendra Singh Dursawat made a presentation on "water management" for Karaikal.

Field visit

Lt Governor Kiran Bedi directed officials of science, technology and, environment and agriculture (Hydrogeologists) to carry out regular inspections of water-consuming industries. The inspection will check on the water management systems, metering of borewells and withdrawal of permitted quantity of water.

Lieutenant Governor Kiran Bedi inspecting water-consuming industries in the Union Territory on Saturday | EXPRESS

Lt Governor for water conservation

EXPRESS NEWS SERVICE
@ Puducherry

LIEUTENANT Governor Kiran Bedi on Saturday exhorted water-consuming industries to ensure improvement in water recharge and reduce consumption to maintain water table.

After visiting the water-consuming industries to check their compliance on water management, the Lt Governor directed officials of Science, Technology and Environment and Agriculture (Hydrogeologists) to jointly carry out regular inspections of water-consuming industries. The inspection will check on the water management systems, metering of borewells and withdrawal of permitted quantity of water. The officials were also instructed to find out if all the other conditions imposed in the consent order are strictly adhered to.

She advised Aravind Eye Hospital to adopt technology to monitor the water level so as to regulate the usage of water within the permissible threshold.

She also advised that, instead of discharging treated non-potable water into the drain, it could be utilised in chemical or plastic industries for the cooling towers.

Bedi: Rope in Dredging Corpn to desilt harbour mouth under CSR scheme

When Quizzed, Officials Cite Lack Of Fund As Reason

Lieutenant governor Kiran Bedi inspecting water at Lake during the weekend rounds on Saturday

Lieutenant Governor Kiran Bedi with a delegation of students and faculty of the US-based Iowa University during her weekend visit to a lake to work out steps for its makeover in Puducherry on Saturday

The new INDIAN EXPRESS   2 8 JAN 2018

Maintain, clean Kanakan lake: L-G

Inspects boats during visit; asks officials to give free passes to students cleaning lake

BAGALAVAN PERIER B
@ Puducherry

AS part of her weekend visit, Lieutenant Governor Kiran Bedi inspected the Kanakan lake again and gave some suggestions to the officials.

She had already inspected the lake on several visits as complaints were raised that the lake water had been spoiled by the drainage from nearby residential area and Indira Gandhi Medical College Hospital nearby.

The bushes, growing abundantly on the lake bund, have become a makeshift bar for tipsy gangs.

During her previous visits, the L-G asked officials to clear the bushes from bund and also stop the mixing of drainage water into the lake. She had a discussion with various department officials and gave suggestions to make the lake a tourist attraction spot.

She asked the PWD to maintain the lake, municipality to clean the lake area, the tourism department to open a canteen and arrange boating, the forest and agriculture department to plant trees and make them grow without any distraction.

On Saturday, she came again to the lake and inspected the three boats brought there for sailing and asked the officials to give free passes for one week to the students involved in the lake-cleaning work.

At the boating inauguration ceremony, she asked the officials to call the local MLA, and respective officials and also ordered installation of LED lights along the footpath made around the lake.

Along the path near the medical college, she asked the college management to fix those lights and in other place and also asked to get help from NGOs to fix lights.

She advised the officials to do the work step by step according to the finance availability. She also asked to use the income from the canteen and boating for the lake development.

Officials from various departments including tourism, forest, agriculture, public works and Oulgaret municipality accompanied her.

Raj Nivas awards for water management

Initiative to recognise clean and green causes, says L-G; honour to be given during all festivals and important occasions

SPECIAL CORRESPONDENT
PUDUCHERRY

The Raj Nivas will institute 'SwachhtaHiSeva Awards' in various categories of water, sanitation and environment management, Lt. Governor Kiran Bedi said on Sunday.

The Lt. Governor, who had focused her weekend bus tour to assess the progress on various projects envisaged under the 'Puducherry Water Rich' Mission at the Sri Lakshmi Narayana Medical College and Pondicherry University, said these awards, which would also recognise clean and green causes, would be given away during all festivals and important occasions and events.

The awardees would be nominated by the team associated with driving the Mission along with the Raj Nivas, such as the District Collector, PWD Chief Engineer, Groundwater Authority, S&T, Rural Development Departments, Puducherry and Oulgaret Municipality officials.

Lt. Governor Kiran Bedi on a bus tour to the suburbs to assess progress of the 'Puducherry Water Rich Mission' on Sunday; right, a pit dug up to harvest water in the Pondicherry University. • SPECIAL ARRANGEMENT

Team Raj Nivas will co-opt some members of the community to short list nominees. The winners would be kept a surprise and revealed only at the event.

Starting this Diwali, all upcoming celebrations at Raj Nivas such as Christmas, Pongal, New Year, or other days like the Republic Day, Youth Day or Women's Day will be designated as occasions to honour community leaders from all walks of life, the Lt. Governor said.

Ms. Bedi, who led a Raj Nivas team and Government officials, said it was encouraging to see the results of past efforts as part of the Mission where the institutions had put in place 35 water harvesting structures ahead of the North East monsoon season in what were water-stressed areas on the outskirts of the city.

Moreover, several firms and individuals had volunteered to support efforts to desilt waterways and recharge about 84 waterbodies including tanks, lakes and ponds.

In the last three months, over 100 water harvesting pits had been readied ahead of the monsoon at the community level, the Raj Nivas said.

By: DT Newspaper – 02\10\20

https://www.dtnext.in/News/TamilNadu/2020/02/10012610/1214256/Bedi-asks-children-to-protect-clean-Kanagan-lake.vpf

Lieutenant Governor of Puducherry Kiran Bedi on her weekend visit to a major water body in neighbouring Reddiarpalayam, on Sunday appreciated the clean environment and asked school children, Kanagan lake, members of voluntary organizations and staff of a research institute to ensure that cleanliness of the lake is maintained Stressing on maintenance of such infrastructure.

Lt. Governor Kiran Bedi enjoying a cultural programme presented by students on the banks of Kanagan lake

Puducherry:
The former IPS officer, who used the bicycle to visit the lake from her office, motivated the young children to take care of the lake as their property.

Responding to her appeal, school children and others and French Institute of Puducherry came forward to take care of the lake by taking upon themselves certain extent of the area.

Kiran Bedi, who used certain Tamil words to ask the children, and others to ensure 'suthamana eri' (clean lake) said, "The lake is our property and the children can use it during weekends or holidays as tourist destinations." She also furnished phone numbers for any police help for security purposes.

Bedi asked the police officials who accompanied her to take care of the visitors. Children presented cultural programmes to welcome the Lieutenant Governor on the banks of the lake.

As the documentation process unfolded, I contacted Shyam - a grade 10 student over a telephone call. He vividly described the work done by his NGO Changemakers of Pondy in cleaning of the lake. Shyam wrote a letter to the Lt. Governor describing the dire situation of the Kanagan Lake. A team headed by Grievance Redressal Officer arrived at the location to assess the lake's condition. It surprised the residents as senior officials began charting a plan to clean the lake. One of the numerous incidents leaving an indelible mark on the student community.

I completed my documentation and survey work on the evening of February 16th, 2021. I met the Lt. Governor Dr. Kiran Bedi at 6.30 PM to submit the report within the given time frame. After the meeting, I proceeded to the internship room for incorporating the necessary changes to the report. Interns gathered for dinner at the residence of Lt. Governor. As I was having dinner with co-interns, a member of the social media team rushed past us with a concerned look. I knew something was not right. We received the news in a few minutes. The President of India recalled the Lt. Governor at a time when the Indian National Congress Government was on the brink of collapse. I was left with disbelief and checked the media to verify the reported news. I, along with co-interns, rushed to the office of Lt. Governor and waited outside the office. Silence loomed over Raj Nivas. I heard the sounds of barricades being moved and gates being closed as members of the Congress party surrounded the residence of Lt. Governor. We were not ready to leave the place without meeting our great teacher Dr. Kiran Bedi.

I was doubtful of the scheduled lecture as part of the Intern Lecture Series due to the fast-unfolding administrative changes when our Guru Dr. Kiran Bedi called us into the office, looked at me, and said, "Son — you are presenting on Kanagan Lake; I will not leave Puducherry until all your lectures are complete." Misty-eyed but with firm conviction, I decided to make the best use of the historical opportunity, perhaps the last at the iconic dining hall of Raj Nivas. I immediately compiled a set of 17 pictures. There was no scope for making a poster in the rush of things when I rang the alarm bells back at home through my parents - Dr. Kathirvel and Mrs. Arthy Lakshmi. Staff arrived at 1.30 AM with the Poster and other printouts from my hometown - Namakkal before the presentation at 9.30 AM. I carried a big banner and leaflets for distribution to the surprise of others. Interns assembled at the Durbar Hall to receive specially chosen books from People's Governor Dr. Kiran Bedi. Amongst the interns, I was chosen to be the first student to receive a book. My inner voice echoed that ma'am would select Mahatma Gandhi's Biography from the collection of books. Surprising moments followed as ma'am lifted Mahatma Gandhi's book and gave it with the following words "Mahatma to Mahatma." The end of our internships became moments of eternal joy for the student family. We were considered as the family members of the Lt. Governor whose infinite care and concern for students remain enshrined in our lives.

Flipping the pages of Mahatma Gandhi's Biography received from Lt. Governor Dr. Kiran Bedi

INTERN LECTURE SERIES

SPEAKER: Krithik Kailash

About the Speaker

Krithik Kailash is an Undergraduate Law Student at Christ University. Inspired by Dr. APJ Abdul Kalam's life , this individual focused on Self- development - preparing towards a vision of a developed India.

Krithik believes in the words of Dr.APJ.Abdul Kalam that :

> *" The ignited mind of a youth is the most powerful resource on Planet Earth"*

In September 2019 – Krithik's inner calling for a mentor , guide brought to him: the opportunity to Intern at the office of Dr. Kiran Bedi , Lieutenant Governor of Puducherry. The work profiles handled by Krithik at Raj Nivas are Jal Shakti Abhiyan , Mission Water Rich Puducherry , Mission Green Puducherry , Outreach Programs – Rural Education and Field visits. He has assisted data assimilation for a research on Water Rich Puducherry , University of Harvard.

Krithik is passionate about reading books and The Bhagavad Gita has greatly influenced his thought process. Krithik aspires to a carreer in law to use Public Interest Litigation as a redressal mechanism. Krithik is indebted to his parents for strong values of spirituality and inner strength.Krithik is an avid football and tennis player.

About the topic

Revitalization of Kanagan lake highlights the importance of field visits that were integral for transformation of this water body. Story trails would weave successful collaboration of Team Puducherry. The leadership of Dr. Kiran Bedi created a synergy which led to the revitalization of the Kanagan Lake. This leadership created further leaders in departments, communities to take on collective responsibility. The consistent effort of the people, a scientific approach combined with practical ideas during the cleaning of lake was fundamental in achieving the goal. The cleaning of Kanagan Lake forged a team of volunteers which created an impact on the community to voluntarily participate in reviving lakes and ponds.

'About the Speaker' as part of Intern Lecture Series at Durbar Hall

After the meeting at Durbar Hall, I began my speech on the revitalization of Kanagan Lake:

Intern Lecture Series

Good afternoon, ma'am

Inspired by Dr. Kalam's belief that "learning gives you creativity, creativity leads to thinking, thinking gives you knowledge, and knowledge makes you great," I delved into his life as a 10-year-old boy, how his teacher Siva Subramaniyam Iyer inspired him, and his encounters with other great individuals. I prayed to God that one day I, too, would meet a personality who would inspire me. In September 2019, an unexpected thought came to my mind, "Go to Puducherry; you will get the Opportunity." And that's how I had the privilege to meet my great teacher, Dr. Kiran Bedi madam. With utmost respect, I begin the presentation on the Kanagan model.

The Kanagan Lake, founded by the French government in 1911, is one of the oldest freshwater lakes in the Puducherry region. Neglecting the lake was attributed to two main reasons - urbanization and the direct flow of sewage water into it. In 2016, after Dr. Kiran Bedi took oath as the Lt. Governor of Puducherry, a complaint was received during the first Open House regarding the dire condition of the lake. Dr. Bedi's response was to collaborate with the community and begin working towards its restoration. This picture portrays how Corporate Social Responsibility (CSR) was enlisted to contribute to the cleaning efforts through Mission Water-Rich Puducherry, showcasing how Dr. Bedi utilized various resources to benefit the community. The presentation features 16 pictures with lessons for our lives, and this specific image emphasized the significance of regular reviews for every mission and meeting.

This picture shows the inspiring story of 13-year-old Shyam. He is one of Team Raj Nivas's staunchest supporters and founded the NGO "Changemakers of Pondicherry" while studying in grade X. When asked about his team's size, he proudly shared that he started alone and gradually convinced three passing students about the lake's importance, expanding his team to 13 members. This showcases the remarkable leadership of Dr. Kiran Bedi, who has not only created young leaders but also ignited the youth's vision, making them protectors and guardians of the lake. On December 30, 2017, the lake was plagued with water hyacinth mainly due to the flow of sewage water. However, by January 20, 2018, considerable progress in cleaning the lake was noticed. On February 3, 2018, the lake was open for boating, and on July 24, 2019, we witnessed a clean and rejuvenated Kanagan Lake. This picture teaches us the importance of community participation and how one great leader can empower and inspire young minds to bring about positive change.

The Lt. Governor has tweeted about the successful restoration of biodiversity in Kanagan Lake. This achievement is a result of collaborative work, where people have been economically involved, making them the guardians of the lake. Now, the lake offers seating areas for families to visit, a dream project that all of us have worked on. Activities like chanting of Bhagavad Geeta and tree plantation have added to the beauty of this wonderful lake. In a recorded video during a field visit, the Lt. Governor emphasizes the importance of collective responsibility and division of tasks among young children, coordinated with the beat officer. Among all these accomplishments, the Swachhata Hi Seva Awards signify the significance of appreciation, with certificates bearing Lt. Governor's signature, cherished by the people of Puducherry. This picture provides a clear view of Kanagan Lake, a mission that started in 2016 and was successfully completed in 2019.

I end with Thirukkural, written 2500 years back;

வெள்ளத் தனைய மலர்நீட்டம் மாந்தர்தம்
உள்ளத் தனைய துயர்வு.

Thiruvalluvar's wisdom resonates in the saying that the lily flower always blossoms, regardless of the depth or condition of the water. Similarly, with unwavering determination and a clear goal, even seemingly impossible tasks can be achieved. Over the past five years, Team Raj Nivas, under the leadership of the People's Governor, has faced numerous challenges, but every mission has been undertaken with great vision and dedication. This commitment has left a lasting impression on the hearts of the entire team, the interns, and the people of Puducherry. We promise you, ma'am, that wherever we go and whatever we do, we will carry forward the fame and the transformative revolution that Puducherry has witnessed under your tenure.

Speech Ends.

Dr. Kiran Bedi - What are you? My son or grandson?

Sounds of laughter and smiles…

Intern Krithik Kailash - "Son ma'am…"

Dr. Kiran Bedi - That means I am still a young mother. Any parent would be so proud of a boy like you.

Intern Krithik Kailash: Thank you ma'am

Comptroller Asha Gupta: For us, Krithik was like a database, we just had to tell him one word, and he would be ten words ahead, so there was a lot of interest in telling, because we got back so much and joy of giving was utmost…every time I just needed to call him, whether Snighdha came for the Harvard Project, and I asked him if he is free; he used to immediately rush to Raj Nivas.

My last two weeks of internship included cycling at Auroville on a cool Sunday morning remains to be a fresh experience. A batch of interns left early in the morning to the Auroville forest as Lt. Governor's cavalcade arrived a few minutes later for the weekend visit. We visited a picturesque house with nature's abundant blessings for a quick breakfast as we explored the Auroville forest where temperatures are cooler as a result of infinite trees protected by the Government. The Olunder Lake visit was a review of the work undertaken by the Public Works Department and Team Raj Nivas. The lake now has its marine ecosystem flourishing with its water pure and sustainable for life elements. We cycled twice around the lake as the Lt. Governor awarded the student volunteers for their participation in cleaning the lake. A local resident brought a big fish to show the positive environmental impact as a result of Mission Water Rich Puducherry. Planting the saplings and further discussions on the need for preservation and conservation of environment were the major learnings from the field visit.

Group picture with our Internship Certificate at the Durbar Hall of Raj Nivas

Individual Career Guidance by Lt. Governor Dr. Kiran Bedi to the Intern family

Signing of the Internship Certificate by Lt.Governor Dr. Kiran Bedi

Seat of Lt. Governor in the backdrop

Receiving the Internship Certificate from Lt. Governor Dr. Kiran Bedi [2019]

Receiving the Internship Certificate from Lt. Governor Dr. Kiran Bedi [2019]

Chapter 14

TWITTER SPEECH

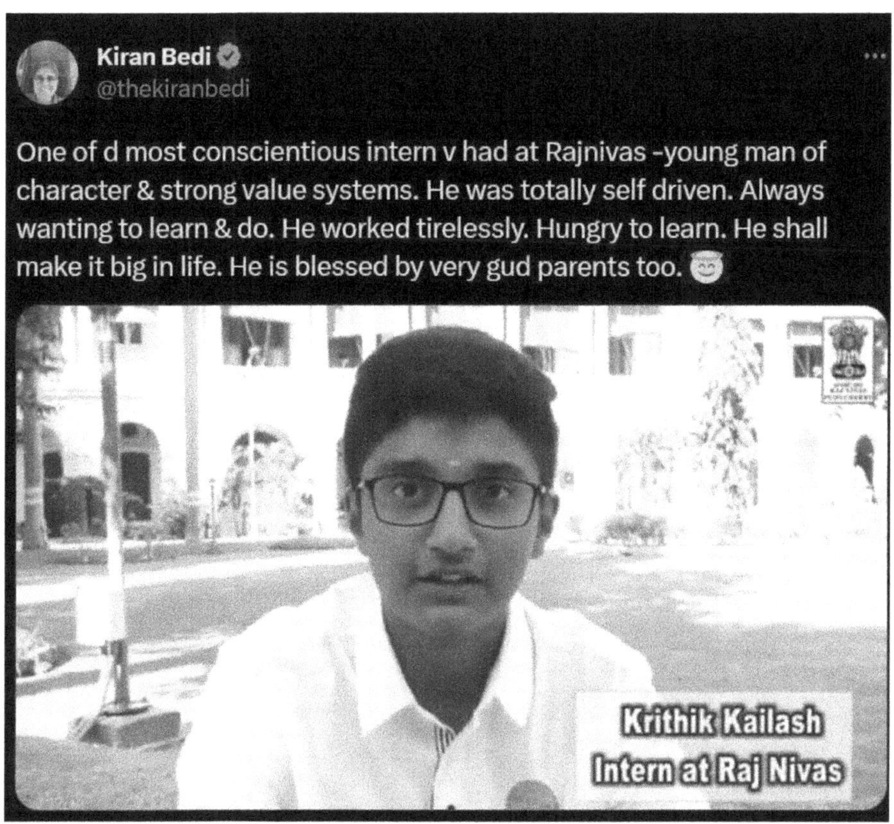

SPEECH:

"My Internship Experience at Raj Nivas has been a unique one. I have learned that whatever I do, I should do it with passion, dedication, energy, and enthusiasm. Few of the qualities I take away from here are that I have improved on my communication skills, built my confidence, learned to help, work, and progress more. I have learned the importance of teamwork; in a team, you require trust, empowerment, and accountability. I could realize that under the leadership of our Lt. Governor, Team Raj Nivas is not just a team, it's a family, it's People's Nivas, and most of all, we have a People's Governor. The success stories of open house and the Puducherry governance model will be etched in our history and act as a role model for every government.

"The Mission Green Puducherry, Water Rich Puducherry, Prosperous Puducherry, initiatives led by our Lt. Governor, have not just made Puducherry prosperous, but also joyful and happy. I have always been thankful to God that I am born in such a vibrant democracy. Besides its culture, tradition, and diversity, India has produced great leaders steering our nation forward. Leaders like our Lt. Governor have inspired millions of people across our country and defined life's very purpose. To sum up my internship experience at Raj Nivas, I am reminded of a Thirukkural written by Saint Thiruvalluvar that none can defeat a speaker who is good, efficient, and tireless in life. Thank you so much, Lt. Governor Ma'am, and Team Raj Nivas."

The unique functioning style of the Lt. Governor as India's most renowned and decorated police officer made the internship a thrilling experience for the intern family. We were provided all three meals prepared at the Governor's Palace. In the following days after the lecture series, People's Governor Dr. Kiran Bedi stamping her mark in Puducherry, left for New Delhi with the abundant blessings of mother nature as it rained heavily during the departure after which the clouds became clear. I reached back to my hometown - Namakkal, with a certificate in hand along with a lifetime experience indebted to our beloved and devoted Guru Dr. Kiran Bedi and Team Raj Nivas. After the internship at Raj Nivas, I worked with a new platform called Demonstrative Learning which integrates the life of Dr. Kiran Bedi. Further, I organized multiple virtual meets in Zoom for the interns to share their progress with Dr. Kiran Bedi. We remain connected through a WhatsApp Group as part of the treasured relationship of a teacher and student built over a period of time.

Seeking the blessings of Sri Perumal [Lord Vishnu] – Presiding Deity at Raj Nivas as gates close for intern family.

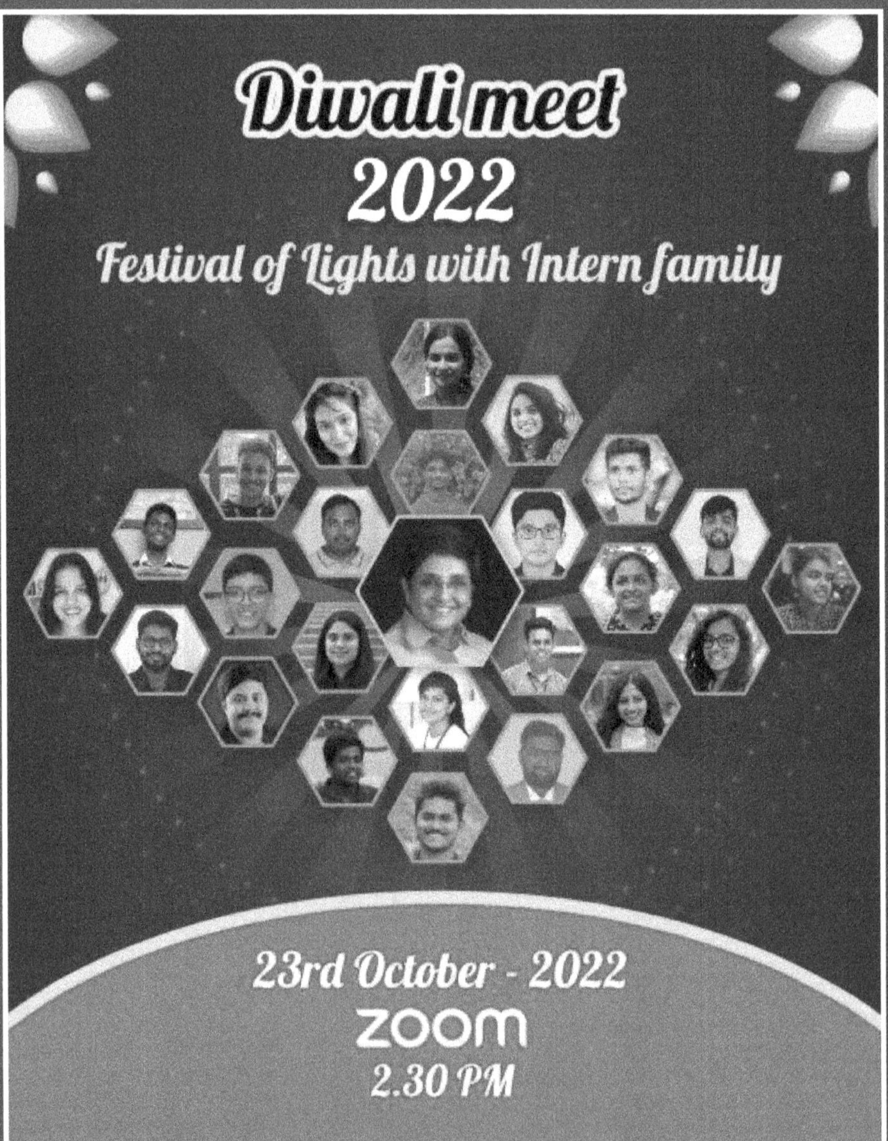

Organized a virtual internship meet – 2022

Speaking on the tenure of Lt. Governor Dr. Kiran Bedi at a school event in Tiruppur, Tamil Nadu.

Online meeting with Dr. Kiran Bedi in the presence of Chief Executive at Demonstrative Learning Mrs. Saina Bharucha and Sister K. Deeksha.

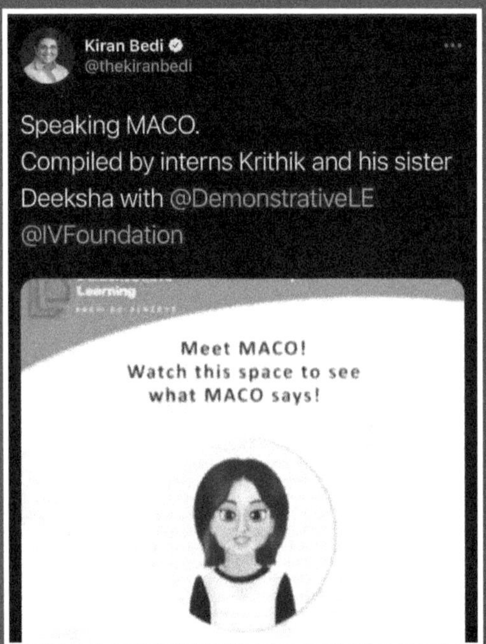

Working along with Sister K. Deeksha for Demonstrative Learning – a virtual platform integrating the life of Dr. Kiran Bedi.

INSIGHT:

Working on the book 'People's Governor'

NEWSPAPER SOURCES

1. Deccan Herald - April 01, 2020,
    https://www.deccanherald.com/national/south/lockdown-rules-section-144-should-be-strictly-observed-kiran-bedi-819860.html

2. NDTV [PTI] – April 26th, 2020,
    https://www.ndtv.com/india-news/india-coronavirus-lockdown-free-rice-distribution-to-60-beneficiaries-completed-in-puducherry-kiran—2218441

3. Times of India – May 6th, 2020,
    https://timesofindia.indiatimes.com/city/puducherry/kiran-bedi-asks-people-to-share-info-on-illegal-liquor-sale-in-puducherry/articleshow/75581663.cms

4. United News of India – July 1st, 2020
    http://www.uniindia.com/~/pondy-lg-greets-doctors-on-national-doctors-day/States/news/2060784.html.

5. The Hindu – August 10th, 2020
    https://www.thehindu.com/news/national/tamil-nadu/bedi-appeals-to-elected-representatives/article32312080.ece

6. Medical Dialogues, 21st August, 2020
    https://medicaldialogues.in/news/health/bring-all-private-medical-college-on-board-for-covid-treatment-kiran-bedi-asks-pm-modi-home-minister-68804

7. Deccan Herald – August 23rd, 2020
    https://www.deccanherald.com/national/south/rise-in-covid-19-cases-in-india-due-to-flouting-of-norms-by-people-bedi-876838.html

8. ET Government – September 3rd, 2020
    *https://government.economictimes.indiatimes.com/news/
    governance/puducherry-lt-governor-kiran-bedi-appoints-top-ias-
    officer-to-check-covid-19situation/77904026#:~:text=Drafting%20
    a%20new%20mechanism%20to,pandemic%20situation%20in%20
    the%20region.*